BETTER BYLAWS

Creating Effective Rules for Your Nonprofit Board

SECOND EDITION

PROPERTY OF

DEC 2 2 2010

THE FOUNDATION CTR

by
D. Benson Tesdahl, Esq.

BOARDSOURCE®
Building Effective Nonprofit Boards

Library of Congress Cataloging-in-Publication Data

Tesdahl, D. Benson, 1932-

Better bylaws : creating effective rules for your nonprofit board / D. Benson Tesdahl. -- 2nd ed.

p. cm.

Rev. ed. of: The nonprofit board's guide to bylaws.

ISBN 1-58686-118-2

1. Nonprofit organizations--Law and legislation--United States. 2. Corporate governance--Law and legislation--United States. 3. Nonprofit organizations--United States--By-laws. 4. Directors of corporations--United States--Handbooks, manuals, etc. I. Tesdahl, D. Benson, 1932- The nonprofit board's guide to bylaws II. Title.

KF1388.5.T47 2010
346.73'064--dc22   2010014956

© 2010 BoardSource.
First Printing, May 2010
ISBN 1-58686-118-2

Published by BoardSource
1828 L Street, NW, Suite 900
Washington, DC 20036

This publication may not be reproduced without permission. Permission can be obtained by completing a request for permission form located at www.boardsource.org. Revenue from publications sales ensures the capacity of BoardSource to produce resources and provide services to strengthen the governing boards of nonprofit organizations. Copies of this book and all other BoardSource publications can be ordered by calling 800-883-6262. Discounts are available for bulk purchases.

The views in each BoardSource publication are those of its author, and do not represent official positions of BoardSource or its sponsoring organizations. Information and guidance in this book is provided with the understanding that BoardSource is not engaged in rendering professional opinions. If such opinions are required, the services of an attorney should be sought.

BOARDSOURCE®
Building Effective Nonprofit Boards

BoardSource was established in 1988 by the Association of Governing Boards of Universities and Colleges (AGB) and Independent Sector (IS). Prior to this, in the early 1980s, the two organizations had conducted a survey and found that although 30 percent of respondents believed they were doing a good job of board education and training, the rest of the respondents reported little, if any, activity in strengthening governance. As a result, AGB and IS proposed the creation of a new organization whose mission would be to increase the effectiveness of nonprofit boards.

With a lead grant from the Kellogg Foundation and funding from five other donors, BoardSource opened its doors in 1988 as the National Center for Nonprofit Boards with a staff of three and an operating budget of $385,000. On January 1, 2002, BoardSource took on its new name and identity. These changes were the culmination of an extensive process of understanding how we were perceived, what our audiences wanted, and how we could best meet the needs of nonprofit organizations.

Today BoardSource is the premier voice of nonprofit governance. Its highly acclaimed products, programs, and services mobilize boards so that organizations fulfill their missions, achieve their goals, increase their impact, and extend their influence. BoardSource is a 501(c)(3) organization.

BoardSource provides

- resources to nonprofit leaders through workshops, training, and an extensive Web site (www.boardsource.org)

- governance consultants who work directly with nonprofit leaders to design specialized solutions to meet an organization's needs

- the world's largest, most comprehensive selection of material on nonprofit governance, including a large selection of books and CD-ROMs

- an annual conference that brings together approximately 900 governance experts, board members, and chief executives and senior staff from around the world

For more information, please visit our Web site at www.boardsource.org, e-mail us at mail@boardsource.org, or call us at 800-883-6262.

Have You Used These BoardSource Resources?

THE GOVERNANCE SERIES

1. *Ten Basic Responsibilities of Nonprofit Boards, Second Edition*
2. *Legal Responsibilities of Nonprofit Boards, Second Edition*
3. *Financial Responsibilities of Nonprofit Boards, Second Edition*
4. *Fundraising Responsibilities of Nonprofit Boards, Second Edition*
5. *The Nonprofit Board's Role in Mission, Planning, and Evaluation, Second Edition*
6. *Structures and Practices of Nonprofit Boards, Second Edition*

OTHER BOOKS

The Nonprofit Policy Sampler, Second Edition

The Nonprofit Legal Landscape

Managing Conflicts of Interest: A Primer for Nonprofit Boards, Second Edition

The Nonprofit Board Answer Book: A Practical Guide for Board Members and Chief Executives, Second Edition

The Nonprofit Chief Executive's Ten Basic Responsibilities

Chief Executive Transitions: How to Hire and Support a Nonprofit CEO

Assessment of the Chief Executive

The Board Chair Handbook, Second Edition

Getting the Best from Your Board: An Executive's Guide to a Successful Partnership

Moving Beyond Founder's Syndrome to Nonprofit Success

The Source: Twelve Principles of Governance That Power Exceptional Boards

Exceptional Board Practices: The Source in Action

Fearless Fundraising for Nonprofit Boards, Second Edition

Navigating the Organizational Lifecycle: A Capacity-Building Guide for Nonprofit Leaders

Generating Buzz: Strategic Communications for Nonprofit Boards

Understanding Nonprofit Financial Statements, Third Edition

Transforming Board Structure: Strategies for Committees and Task Forces

The Board Building Cycle: Nine Steps to Finding, Recruiting, and Engaging Nonprofit Board Members, Second Edition

Culture of Inquiry: Healthy Debate in the Boardroom

Chief Executive Succession Planning: Essential Guidance for Boards and CEOs, Second Edition

Meeting, and Exceeding Expectations: A Guide to Successful Nonprofit Board Meetings, Second Edition

Who's Minding the Money? An Investment Guide for Nonprofit Board Members, Second Edition

DVDs

Meeting the Challenge: An Orientation to Nonprofit Board Service

Speaking of Money: A Guide to Fundraising for Nonprofit Board Members

ONLINE ASSESSMENTS

Board Self-Assessment

Assessment of the Chief Executive

Executive Search — Needs Assessment

For an up-to-date list of publications and information about current prices, membership, and other services, please call BoardSource at 800-883-6262 or visit our Web site at www.boardsource.org. For consulting services, please e-mail us at consulting@boardsource.org or call 877-892-6293.

CONTENTS

The CD-ROM in the back of this book provides bylaws templates and policies appropriate for most nonprofit organizations. There are three bylaws templates: one for organizations with self-perpetuating boards of directors, one for organizations with formal voting memberships, and one for charitable subsidiaries or "supporting organizations" controlled by parent entities. There are three sample policies: a conflict-of-interest policy, a whistleblower protection policy, and a record retention and document destruction policy. In addition, there is an example of articles of incorporation, although it should not be used without consulting state law and the advice of legal counsel. The material on the CD-ROM may be downloaded and customized.

INTRODUCTION

Bylaws are significant written rules by which an organization is governed. With minor exceptions, they largely follow a similar structure in all nonprofit organizations, since the mission of the organization does not ordinarily affect the structure of the governance document. Thus, the overview and principles offered in this book will be applicable largely to most nonprofit boards.

Although boards formalize their governance rules in bylaws, these helpful rules are frequently neglected and sometimes even ignored in the rush to get business done quickly. For many reasons, however, nonprofit organizations should pay more careful attention to bylaws. Take, for example, the question of the size of the board. An unnecessarily large and unwieldy board of directors can impair an organization's ability to make decisions and meet new challenges, while an entrenched group of long-time directors might prevent a nonprofit from adapting to change. Bylaws are the tools with which organizations address the questions surrounding directors on the board, specifying their number and any term limits.

During governing controversies, bylaws have particular importance. These disputes may have many forms: a board member who is voted out of office seeks reinstatement, a dissident group within the organization attempts to gain control of the board, or a faction mounts a legal challenge to a board decision. In these difficult situations, carefully crafted bylaws and adherence to them can help ensure the fairness of board decisions and provide protection against legal challenges.

The laws of a few states require that membership categories, board selection, and other issues be stated in the articles of incorporation. In most states, however, details about governance are put solely in the bylaws where they can be amended without the need to file such amendments with the state. In either case, bylaws expand on the articles of incorporation as necessary and typically perform at least three important functions:

- First, they determine how an organization is structured. Specifically, they tell the board how the governance of the entity is intended to be structured and cover lines of authority within the organization, but they do not cover the structure of the professional staff. For example, most bylaws specify whether an organization has membership categories, define the duties of officers and directors, and identify standing board committees. An important function of bylaws (if this matter is not covered in the articles) is to specify how directors are selected.

- Second, bylaws — along with state law — determine the rights of participants in the structure, such as the rights of members to be notified of meetings and to vote, the rights of directors or officers whom others want to remove from office, and the rights of directors and officers to indemnification for costs incurred in performing their duties.

- Third, bylaws determine many procedures by which rights can be exercised. For example, bylaws may require a certain form of notice for meetings, or they may specify whether board meetings can be held by telephone or elections conducted by mail.

The choice among alternative operational bylaws can directly affect how organizations resolve issues. One challenge frequently facing organizations with very large boards of directors, for example, is the desire to have faster and more efficient decision making. These organizations may require a reduction in the number of directors, establishment of an executive committee, creation or improved operation of standing committees, modification of day-to-day operations, or a combination of these alternatives. A number of bylaws and procedures may be relevant to achieve these ends.

This book provides a basic definition of bylaws and an overview of the issues and areas bylaws should address. For experienced board and staff members, this material may be familiar; for others, it will be new. Throughout the book, examples are used to illustrate the relationship between state law and bylaws. (All examples in this book use hypothetical organizations and people, none of which are intended to reflect any real-life organization or person with similar names.) Findings from a survey by BoardSource's *Nonprofit Governance Index 2007* provide empirical data about how nonprofits handle certain issues and may help boards choose among alternative bylaws provisions.

A word of caution: While sample bylaws provisions are provided electronically on the included CD-ROM, this book is not intended to be used as a "do-it-yourself" guide to drafting bylaws. Bylaws can draw on someone else's example, but they need to be tailored to an organization's specific contexts. Moreover, there are legal requirements that differ from one jurisdiction to another. Because nonprofit organizations and state laws vary widely, it is advisable to consult an attorney who is knowledgeable about nonprofit corporate law before adopting or revising bylaws.

PART 1
BYLAWS IN CONTEXT

Most nonprofit organizations are legally organized as corporations. By going through the incorporation process, which involves meeting a number of legal requirements and submitting articles of incorporation to a state government, a group of individuals who work together for a specific purpose can create a corporation. The resulting legal entity is separate from the individuals forming it. A corporation has powers, obligations (such as the ability to enter into contracts, borrow money, and pay taxes), and liabilities that are ordinarily distinct from those of its incorporators, officers, directors, and/or members. The corporate form is therefore a good means of limiting the personal liability of directors.

This book focuses on the bylaws of nonprofit corporations. For unincorporated organizations, "articles of association" often serve as both the organizing document and the bylaws for internal governance. Such articles can have even more significance for internal governance because they are often the only written rules and there is often no accompanying state law authority for the governance of unincorporated entities.

Bylaws contain the primary key governance details of the organization and are essentially a contract between the corporation and its directors, officers, and dues-paying members (if any). Bylaws discuss a wide range of governance issues, including

- which stakeholders in the organization have voting power and how they can cast those votes

- how the governing body and its officers are elected and removed

- how meetings are called and what percentage of eligible attendees are sufficient for the meeting to be lawful

- whether it is possible to vote on a matter by written ballot or in some other means other than a formal meeting

- how committees are formed and what the scope of their authority will be

- when and how directors and officers are indemnified for any costs they incur in performing their duties

- and any number of other key governance provisions

Consequently, if a dispute arises regarding any aspect of the governance of a nonprofit corporation, the key place that courts will look for the answer is the bylaws.

In discussing bylaws, it is important to understand the definitions, functions, and relationships among state corporate laws, articles of incorporation, board resolutions, and policies as background to the bylaws themselves.

STATE CORPORATE LAW

The highest authority governing nonprofit corporation documents is the state nonprofit corporation act. Neither the articles of incorporation nor the bylaws may violate any provision of state corporate law. If they do, any provision in violation of such law is void. For example, if state corporate law provides that the maximum single term of office for any officer is three years, a provision in the bylaws allowing for four-year terms of office is illegal and can be challenged. Therefore, it is critically important for those operating and advising nonprofit corporations to be familiar with the requirements of state corporate law.

Most states have a separate nonprofit corporation act (although a few states merely have a general corporation statute that applies to both nonprofit entities and for-profit entities). The corporation statutes provide very specific requirements for the contents of articles of incorporation. Because the articles of incorporation must be filed with the state, the contents of those articles will be carefully reviewed by a state official to ensure that they match the requirements of state law.

By contrast, the specific contents of bylaws are often not specified by state law, and, moreover, bylaws are never filed with the state, which means that no state official checks their content against state law. Although it is rare, a few state nonprofit corporation laws are fairly brief and general (e.g., Maryland), thereby allowing a nonprofit to have almost any bylaws governance procedures it desires. (In some cases where the nonprofit statute is very brief, it may refer to the for-profit corporation statute and adopt those for-profit provisions by analogy to the extent they apply.) A few state laws are very detailed and sometimes have specific bylaws governance requirements and limitations for how to give notice, how to call meetings, and how to elect and remove directors and officers. Most state laws tend to take a middle ground and provide a minimum default rule "unless otherwise stated in the bylaws," which then allows nonprofits to deviate from the default rule if they care to do so.

Many nonprofits are unaware that they have bylaws provisions that are in technical violation of state corporate law, and they sometimes operate for many years under such provisions without any adverse consequence. As noted above, the reason is that the bylaws are never filed with the state government, and consequently, there is no government official who is monitoring bylaws compliance with state law. Unless a board member or dues-paying member of the nonprofit happens to notice the bylaws problem and raises it as an issue, it is possible for nonprofits to operate for decades with bylaws that violate state law. And in many instances, operating in violation of the bylaws causes no real harm because many nonprofit board decisions are unanimous and without controversy. For example, if a nonprofit board votes to honor the service of a past board member, and if that vote is taken in technical violation of state law, there is no real harm done and nobody is going to complain about such a violation. Nevertheless, it is always a best practice to ensure that bylaws comply with state law and that you follow those bylaws as written.

The primary way that bylaws problems come to light is when an adverse action is taken by a nonprofit (such as removal of a director or removal of a dues-paying member), in which case the affected person often hires legal counsel, who then is able to challenge the action as being in violation of state law. In such cases, it is sometimes possible to get a state court to order the nonprofit to reinstate the person or to otherwise reverse the board's decision. Here are two examples (of fictitious organizations) that illustrate when violations of state law do and do not make a meaningful difference.

EXAMPLE 1

State law says that notice of a board meeting can be delivered only by regular mail, facsimile, or hand delivery. The National Oil and Gas Association, a nonprofit trade association, has bylaws that also list electronic mail as a method for delivering notice of meetings, which is contrary to state law. The association regularly delivers notice of its board meetings to all directors by electronic mail, and those directors have for years attended board meetings without objecting to the form of the notice. Although the association has bylaws and a notice procedure that are in violation of state law, it hasn't experienced any objections by directors. The lack of objections will most likely result in the prior board meetings and the decisions made at them being upheld, particularly if no adverse action was taken at any of those meetings.

EXAMPLE 2

State law says that notice of a board meeting can be delivered only by regular mail, facsimile, or hand delivery. The Environmental Research Society, a nonprofit educational charity, has bylaws that also list electronic mail as a method for delivering notice of meetings, which is contrary to state law. The chair of the board of the society sends out an e-mail notice of a board meeting at which it is proposed that board member Sally be removed from office due to misconduct. Sally does not attend the board meeting, but the other directors meet on the appointed day and vote to remove her. Sally could challenge her removal on the grounds that there was no lawfully called meeting because notice of the meeting was given in violation of state law. The lesson to be learned is never to take any adverse action or potentially controversial action without carefully studying both state law and the bylaws to ensure that they are followed to the letter.

ARTICLES OF INCORPORATION

Although it is possible in some situations to obtain tax exemption for a trust, a limited liability company, or an unincorporated association, the vast majority of nonprofits form themselves as corporations. This is done by preparing articles of incorporation.

The articles of incorporation are filed with the appropriate state office, which is often a department within the secretary of state's office. They typically include the new organization's full legal name; a general statement of purpose, which must comply with federal tax laws if the entity is to be tax exempt; a provision for the disposition of assets if the organization is dissolved; the name and address of a "registered agent" to receive lawsuits and official mail on behalf of the entity; and the names and addresses of the initial board of directors. If the organization is to be a section 501(c)(3) charity, it is also common to put into the articles certain provisions limiting the amount of lobbying that may be conducted, prohibiting any political campaign intervention by the organization, and prohibiting any private inurement (or benefit). One or more incorporators sign the articles before they are filed.

Although the laws of many states permit some rules for the governance of the corporation to be set out in either the articles or the bylaws, the articles of incorporation should be as general as possible and should contain only the minimum that is required by state law. (See Appendix 1 for a sample.) The goal is to have a general and flexible document that will not need to be amended, since any changes to the articles of incorporation require filing special paperwork with the state and paying a filing fee.

Many states have a sample template for articles of incorporation that is available on the state's Web site. However, that template contains only the minimum language required by state law, and it will almost never contain special federal tax exemption language that is sometimes required by the Internal Revenue Code in order to obtain IRS recognition of tax exemption. Therefore, state sample templates of articles of incorporation must be used with caution because they are almost never sufficient by themselves to qualify an organization for federal tax exemption.

Appendix 1 contains an example of articles of incorporation for a section 501(c)(3) charity that would pass muster for tax exemption with the IRS, although state law may require additional provisions. Nonprofit organizations should always consult their state Web site to determine the format and content for articles of incorporation that are to be filed in their state. In addition, it is always advisable to have the assistance of legal counsel when drafting nonprofit articles of incorporation.

BYLAWS

The bylaws, which are more easily revised and amended than the articles of incorporation, and which do not need to be filed with the state, should deal with more specific issues regarding corporate structure and governance. The bylaws are subordinate to the articles of incorporation, and if there is a conflict, the articles always prevail. Therefore, it is essential that operating nonprofit organizations be familiar with the contents of the articles of incorporation so that the articles and bylaws are never inconsistent. In addition, as noted above, both the articles and the bylaws must be consistent with state corporate laws. Here's an example that illustrates why this consistency is important.

The articles of incorporation of the Professional Nurses Association, a nonprofit professional association, state that the board of directors must have no fewer than nine directors. The bylaws of the association state that the board of directors must have no fewer than seven directors. State law only requires that a board have at least three directors, "unless a greater number is stated in the articles of incorporation or bylaws." In this situation, the association must have a board of at least nine to avoid being in violation of its articles of incorporation, which trump the conflicting bylaws provision requiring only seven directors. The solution to this kind of problem is never to put unnecessary governance details in the articles of incorporation (since most states do not require the upper limit of the board to be stated in the articles) and instead put such information only in the bylaws. In addition, as discussed in part 3 of this book, it is better to list a range for the size of the board (e.g., "not fewer than three nor more than nine"), rather than listing a fixed number of directors. Of course, if state law does not allow a range of directors and instead requires a fixed number, the key is to not put that fixed number in the articles of incorporation, but instead put it in the bylaws.

If a nonprofit organization is going to file for recognition of tax exemption with the Internal Revenue Service, a copy of the bylaws should be appended to that application. (If bylaws have yet to be created, the organization will need to explain in some detail the process for selecting officers and directors so that the IRS is satisfied that there is a reasonable method in place for choosing those who will govern the organization.) The IRS will briefly review the bylaws primarily to ensure that there are governance procedures in place that will preclude an improper private benefit by the governing directors on the board, but the IRS will not analyze the bylaws for compliance with local state law. After recognition of tax exemption is granted, the organizaton simply notifies the IRS on the annual information return (Form 990) that a bylaws change has occurred, but the IRS will not normally review those bylaws changes or determine their propriety. Consequently, nonprofit entities are largely left to police their own bylaws changes, and, most of the time, there is no state or federal official looking over their shoulders to ensure that bylaws match state law.

One common question is whether bylaws are a public document that should be readily shared by a nonprofit. As a matter of law, the general public has no legal right to see the bylaws of an organization. (As a rule, the only documents that many nonprofits are required to share with the public are the Form 990 information return, Form 990-T, and the Application for Recognition of Exemption, also known as Form 1023.) Nevertheless, in the interest of transparency, some nonprofits will post their bylaws on their Web sites, although, in some cases, the bylaws are in a "members only" area. Other nonprofits, however, take the position that the bylaws would be confusing and/or of little interest to the general public, particularly for those who have no right to become dues-paying members of the organization. Consequently, many nonprofits do not make the bylaws available to the public.

In deciding governance policies and the content of bylaws, some nonprofit organizations look to governance guidelines promulgated by various so-called "charity watchdog organizations." While it is true that the general public often puts a great deal of credence in governance guidelines and charitable ratings developed by such organizations, the public should remember that most are self-appointed, private organizations that have no affiliation with state or federal government authority. Thus, their guidelines are not mandatory. Moreover, the governance guidelines of watchdog organizations often far exceed the minimum requirements of both state corporate law and the Internal Revenue Code provisions applicable to nonprofit organizations. Some watchdog guidelines might be impractical or even counterproductive for some organizations to follow. Therefore, it is important to seek legal advice before blindly adopting charity watchdog governance guidelines so that counsel can advise your organization as to which guidelines make sense for your nonprofit and which ones do not.

BOARD RESOLUTIONS

Issues contained in the bylaws should be distinguished from those that are more suitable for board resolutions. Bylaws should state, interpret, or implement the general governance policies of the organization. Board resolutions, separate from the bylaws, are usually raised and voted on at meetings and usually refer to specific actions, such as authorizing the purchase of a building, or interpreting or implementing a provision of the bylaws. The advantage of using resolutions to supplement the bylaws is to provide the board with flexibility and ease of change.

Some states specifically require the adoption of a resolution to authorize certain board actions. Adoption of a resolution should always be reflected in the minutes of the board meeting.

Maintaining a separately indexed chronological record of resolutions that references the initial date of adoption and any subsequent action can prevent time-consuming searches of the minutes for records of board actions and additional debate on matters that have already been addressed. A subject-indexed record of resolutions is especially useful for active, long-standing institutions. Resolutions organized under particular bylaws or policies provide a running, chronological report of previous interpretations to aid current decision making, avoid inconsistency, and make important information readily available to all directors, officers, and staff.

Although resolutions can interpret and supplement the bylaws, a resolution that conflicts with a provision in the bylaws is probably invalid. A simple resolution cannot amend a bylaw unless the proper bylaws amendment procedure is followed. Most state laws have specific requirements for amending bylaws, and bylaws themselves usually have provisions for amendment.

POLICIES

In addition to using resolutions, organizations should develop policies to address some key governance issues that are too detailed to put into bylaws. For example, guidance on staffing and personnel is best collected in a separate personnel manual. Many policies are actually drafted by senior staff members, although some policies may be important enough that they receive final approval by the board or a committee of the board. Corporate policies governing investments, travel, and reimbursement should also be maintained in a separate policy document. If the board decides that a policy is important enough for it to approve, such a policy is often approved in a resolution, since resolutions are the official actions of a board. However, it is also possible for senior managers to be delegated the authority to set some corporate policies without board approval.

Form 990, which is the annual information return filed by most nonprofits, has a section that asks about corporate policies. For the most part, the particular policies asked about are not required by law, and the IRS arguably has no authority to require such policies or to take any adverse action if the policies are not adopted. Nevertheless, it is considered good governance practice to have the policies mentioned in Form 990, which include a conflict-of-interest policy, a whistleblower protection policy, an executive compensation policy, a document retention and destruction policy, and (if applicable) a joint-venture policy. There is no right or wrong content for such policies; a few samples are located in the Appendices to this book.

Nonprofit boards need to develop processes for creating, reviewing and amending these various policies. In most cases, the board of directors or a committee of the board will draft the initial policies, and then the policies themselves will sometimes contain procedures for how the policies are to be amended. Typically, details about how the directors are to develop and amend policy statements are not put in the bylaws. Rather, the creation of corporate policies is an inherent power of directors that does not need to be memorialized in the bylaws.

EXTERNAL PARLIAMENTARY AUTHORITY

Bylaws are not meant to address every procedural question, and most boards develop their own formal or informal procedures to handle the vast majority of situations that arise during meetings. However, where there is an insurmountable conflict at a meeting and the bylaws or board policies do not provide adequate guidance, the board may find it necessary to refer to an external parliamentary authority, such as *Robert's Rules of Order, Newly Revised,* or the *Sturgis Standard Code of Parliamentary Procedure* (see Suggested Resources).

Nonprofit organizations that adopt a parliamentary procedure must do so with a degree of common sense so that meetings do not get bogged down in needlessly formal rules. For example, *Robert's Rules of Order* has grown over the years to nearly 700 pages! Moreover, because *Robert's Rules* were written well before modern nonprofit state corporate laws were developed, they sometimes conflict with current state laws. If an organization were to follow *Robert's Rules* to the letter, it would need a formally trained parliamentarian and a lawyer in attendance at every meeting. That kind of undue formality and procedural minutia is generally not productive and can result in the tail wagging the dog. The board's goal should be to use the simplest procedure possible to have an orderly meeting where people have a fair opportunity to speak and where the matter to be voted on is clearly understood by everyone. Often this can be accomplished simply by the chair exercising strong leadership and by directors exercising common courtesy for one another. However, if the board has reached an impasse on an issue, it may be necessary to adopt some parliamentary procedures if for no other reason than to resolve the issue. It should also be remembered that any votes taken at the meeting (which might include a vote to table the discussion to a future meeting due to a disagreement) should be reflected in the meeting minutes.

PART 2

THE INITIAL BYLAWS — GETTING THE BALL ROLLING

As noted in Part 1, every nonprofit corporation begins its existence by filing articles of incorporation with the state, and that document typically has very little governance information in it other than perhaps to name the initial board of directors. So once the articles of incorporation have been accepted by the state, the next critical step is for the initial directors to draft the initial set of bylaws so that basic governance rules are established for the corporation. Otherwise, there are no rules in place for how to call meetings, what constitutes a quorum, how to elect officers, how to add or remove officers and directors, and all of the many other key governance issues covered later in this book.

It is sometimes easy for the initial directors to get bogged down in drafting the initial bylaws, especially if those directors do not have significant previous experience in working with nonprofit bylaws. In addition, there is sometimes a tendency to try to get the first set of bylaws to be "perfect" and to cover every conceivable governance issue that might arise, which can result in inordinate amounts of time being spent in drafting, redrafting, and debating the initial bylaws. Another problem is that some inexperienced directors blindly borrow a bylaws example found on the Internet or loaned to them by some other nonprofit, even though the example may not be well drafted or may not fit the needs of the new corporation.

FINDING APPROPRIATE SAMPLES

In most cases, a better approach is to start with very basic bylaws that cover major issues surrounding meetings and elections, and then slowly amend those bylaws over time as the nonprofit matures and as new governance issues arise that are not clearly covered by the initial bylaws. The big question is where to find good bylaws examples that will work for the vast majority of new nonprofits and that are internally consistent and satisfy the requirements of most state laws.

Some good examples of basic bylaws that can be used as a starting point and that cover all of the key governance issues faced by most new nonprofit corporations can be found on the CD-ROM that accompanies this book. These sample bylaws have features that are common and that work well for most nonprofits, such as annual elections for officers and directors, a quorum being defined as a majority of the directors, and most decisions being made by a majority vote of a quorum of the directors. However, even the examples included with this book should not be blindly used in their entirety if they have provisions that are not appropriate for the organization.

Another option is to hire experienced legal counsel, who can in most cases create custom bylaws to precisely fit a particular nonprofit's needs and can do so much more efficiently than could inexperienced volunteer directors. In the vast majority of instances, the bylaws obtained from experienced legal counsel are well worth the money spent and will help the organization get off on the right foot and avoid bylaws challenges for many years to come.

Once the initial bylaws have been drafted, the next question is how to get them approved. This creates a "chicken and egg" scenario because until the initial bylaws have been approved, the nonprofit technically has no rules in place on how to call meetings and how to vote. And yet a vote has to be taken to approve the initial bylaws. The normal procedure is for the initial directors named in the articles of incorporation to informally agree among themselves on a convenient date and time to hold the "initial meeting" of the corporation. An agenda is often developed for the meeting by consensus, and that agenda would include approval of the initial bylaws.

At that initial meeting, one of the directors is appointed to act as interim chair and another director is appointed to act as interim secretary to take minutes. The initial directors then call the meeting to order and vote on the various items on the agenda, which typically include approval of the initial bylaws, the election of officers, and the appointment of one or more people to open a bank account and begin work on a tax exemption application with the Internal Revenue Service. Once the initial bylaws have been approved by the initial board, then those bylaws (as may be amended from time to time) govern the conduct of all future meetings.

In some nonprofits, the initial bylaws are so well drafted that they will work for many years, while in other nonprofits, the bylaws are amended one or more times within the first year or two. If bylaws are amended during the first year, it is most likely to be in a nonprofit that intends to have dues-paying members. In such corporations, amendments to the membership sections of the bylaws are often necessary as the initial directors begin to get a better handle on the precise membership categories and membership criteria that will work best for the corporation. Another area in the bylaws that is sometimes amended in the first few years is the list of permanent standing committees that the nonprofit needs to carry out the work of the corporation. Especially in a new nonprofit with an initially small board, the number of standing committees will start small and then later grow in number and complexity as the size of the board and size of the organization grow.

PART 3
KEY BYLAWS CLAUSES

Part 3 examines key issues that nonprofits face when drafting their bylaws, especially in a changing external or internal environment. The discussion includes alternatives for approaching these issues. (See the included CD-ROM for sample bylaws that may be downloaded and customized.)

The following topics are frequently covered in bylaws, although not every organization would need to address every topic. (For example, a corporation with no voting members would not need a "membership" section in the bylaws.) Topics that raise particularly important legal and governance issues are covered in detail.

General

- official name of the organization (which must match the name in the articles of incorporation)

- location of principal office

- statement of purpose

- any limitations required for tax exemption, such as prohibitions against political campaign participation and inurement

- procedure for disposition of assets upon dissolution (which should also be in the articles of incorporation)

Members

- qualifications for membership
- admission procedures
- dues obligations of members
- classes of membership and their rights and privileges
- notice required for membership meetings
- quorum requirements
- frequency of meetings and meeting procedures
- circumstances under which members may be expelled
- voting procedures (including proxies and written ballots)

Board of Directors

- number of members
- qualifications for membership
- terms of office and term limits
- selection process
- process for filling vacancies
- frequency of meetings
- quorum and voting requirements
- meeting procedures (such as action without a meeting and meeting by telephone or using other technology)
- powers of the executive committee (if any)
- other standing committees (if any)
- compensation
- circumstances under which directors may be removed
- director conflict-of-interest procedures

Officers

- qualifications for holding office
- titles and duties of officers
- process for selecting or appointing officers
- terms and term limits
- provision for a chief executive
- circumstances under which officers may be removed

Committees

- standing committees
- creation of other committees and task forces
- scope of authority for and limitations on committees

Fiscal Matters

- audit committee and audits
- fiscal year of the corporation
- indemnification and insurance for officers and directors

Other Issues

- how bylaws are amended
- how articles of incorporation are amended

STATEMENT OF PURPOSE

A clear statement of purpose should express the consensus around which programs are built and implemented. It is best to draft a broad statement in the articles of incorporation, leaving further clarification and refinement for the bylaws. For example, the articles of incorporation might have a brief purposes clause that merely states that the purpose is to "engage in charitable and educational activities in Illinois," while the bylaws might have a mission statement that is much more detailed and indicates scholarships for needy Illinois students desiring to attend college and the provision of textbooks to needy Illinois K-12 students are the primary focus of the organization's programs. Current programs should fall within, and thus carry the authority of, the bylaws purpose statement. As an organization changes, its focus may also change. After crafting a new or revised strategic plan that articulates a significantly changed mission statement, a nonprofit should review and possibly update the purpose statement in its bylaws.

However, one very important caveat is in order. The purposes clause in the articles of incorporation is the clause that always has legal precedence, and any purposes or mission stated in the bylaws should never conflict with or go beyond the general scope of the purposes in the articles of incorporation. If a nonprofit corporation wishes to amend its purposes to add a significant new activity not covered by the scope of its initial articles of incorporation, the proper course of action is to formally amend the articles of incorporation and file that amendment with the state. (If the articles are properly drafted to state very broad purposes, they will rarely need to be amended.)

Another important caveat is that it is not necessary, and often not advisable, to repeat in the bylaws those legal clauses that are required by the IRS to be in the articles of incorporation. In particular, the articles of incorporation of section 501(c)(3) nonprofits are required to have a clause that covers the disposition of assets upon dissolution. Putting that clause in the bylaws only is not sufficient. The reason is that where corporations include the same provisions in both the articles of incorporation and the bylaws, they tend to forget about the articles of incorporation after incorporation is completed, and they tend to only make future amendments to the bylaws, which then makes the two documents inconsistent.

MEMBERS

In practice, membership can mean many things to an organization. In the bylaws, however, it has a very precise meaning with significant implications.

Under state law, a "member" is typically a person (or entity) who pays dues or has more than a nominal connection with the organization and, in return, receives certain membership rights accorded in the bylaws and under state law. Those rights typically include the right to elect and remove officers and directors and the right to amend the bylaws. In other words, members are able to influence the internal affairs of the corporation.

One common point of confusion is worth noting. Some nonprofit organizations tell potential donors that they can become "members" of the organization by making a donation. While there is nothing wrong with doing this, it must be remembered that the term "member" in this latter context is really just a label used as a fundraising technique and is not intended to give the donor any special rights under the bylaws or state law. As used in the discussion below, however, the term "member" is limited to true members with rights under state nonprofit corporation law. Because true members are entitled to certain procedural rights under state law, and because complying with membership notice and meeting procedures sometimes can be quite onerous, it is important to think very carefully before arbitrarily creating one or more classes of members.

Many nonprofit organizations choose not to have members at all. For example, charities that are funded primarily by donations from the general public (rather than from membership dues) often have no need for members. In such a case, the board of directors controls the entire organization and elects any successor board members. This kind of board is called a self-perpetuating board. The advantage of not having members is that electing directors and amending the bylaws is generally much faster and more efficient, since voting power is vested in a relatively small group of individuals (the board of directors) rather than a large number of members who may be spread over a large geographic area. In addition, some nonprofit organizations have members, but specifically choose to give those members either no voting powers or only voting power on an extremely limited number of issues. Under this latter model, most voting power is again vested in the board of directors for efficiency.

By contrast, some nonprofit organizations, including some charities and most trade associations and professional societies, intentionally have a large category of members who pay dues and thus play a major role in funding the organization. In fact, in many trade and professional associations, furthering the profession of the dues-paying members is the key purpose of the organization. In return for their dues payments, the members play a part in organization governance by electing the board of directors, approving amendments to the articles of incorporation and bylaws, and sometimes approving certain other key decisions. (In trade and professional associations, membership sometimes creates a contract right between the association and its members.) The purpose of this structure is to give members a role in major decisions, while allowing the board of directors to continue to be the main decision-making and policy-setting body.

MEMBER REQUIREMENTS AND CLASSES

Although many states require that the articles of incorporation specify whether there will be formal voting members, most states allow the bylaws to contain all the details regarding whether the organization will have such members and the qualifications necessary for members, as well as the relations, rights, and duties of members to each other and to the organization. When stipulating formal membership qualifications, the organization may divide membership into different categories, such as individual, corporate, emeritus, retired, and student. Because of the importance and frequency of issues relating to members, the categories of members and their related voting rights — even if briefly stated in the articles of incorporation — should be reiterated in detail in the bylaws.

If an organization does have one or more classes of voting members, those members are usually entitled to various procedural rights under state law, as well as whatever rights and privileges are stated in the bylaws. For example, members typically are entitled under state law to a certain number of days of prior written notice of member meetings, and the notice may have to contain certain details regarding the subject of the meeting. Thus, an organization with hundreds of members can incur significant costs and expend significant time and effort just sending out meeting notices to all of those members. In addition, voting members must be given the right to cast a vote on all matters designated for member voting in the bylaws, which often include such things as the election of directors, election of officers, and amendments to the bylaws. Thus, for example, making even a relatively minor change to the bylaws may require calling a meeting of all members and sending out notice to all of them (perhaps hundreds or thousands). (One solution to this problem is to have a bylaws provision that allows minor simplification of clauses or the correction of typographical or other errors in the bylaws to be made by the board without any member ratification.) In addition, members who cannot attend a meeting in person are generally allowed to vote by proxy, and tallying those proxies can be very time consuming. If either the content or the timing of member notice is improper for any reason, disgruntled members may successfully challenge the vote taken at that meeting, which can then result in the need to call a replacement meeting with a new round of notices.

For all of the above reasons, decision making in organizations with very large memberships can be and often is relatively slow, cumbersome, and expensive, compared to having all decisions made by a board of directors. Therefore, organizations should think carefully about whether to have members with voting power and, if so, whether those members should be allowed to vote on all major corporate actions or just a narrowly prescribed list of actions. In addition, state law should be consulted to see if it is permissible to have members vote by electronic ballot in lieu of a meeting, which can save considerable time and money.

BOARD OF DIRECTORS

Nonprofit corporations are governed by a board of directors (sometimes called trustees). Indeed, state law requires that there be a board of directors, and it is the body with ultimate decision-making authority and ultimate responsibility for the organization. The bylaws should address the following board-related issues.

NUMBER OF DIRECTORS

Some states require that the bylaws specify the exact number of directors, and many nonprofits feel compelled to specify an exact number of directors even if state law does not require that they do so. The main problem with specifying a precise number of directors is inflexiblity. For example, if the need arises to make the board larger or smaller, there must be a formal meeting called to amend the bylaws, which is generally a slow process. And if vacancies occur on the board, they must be filled quickly in order to avoid being in violation of the bylaws. But many states allow the bylaws to contain a stated "range" of directors (such as "no fewer than three nor more than nine"), which provides much more flexibility and much less need to amend the bylaws as the size of the board expands or contracts. In calculating the number of directors, careful consideration should be given to whether

- the officers are chosen from among the directors

- the officers are directors by virtue of being officers

- the officers are chosen from the general public (or the organization's general membership, if any) but are not also part of the board of directors

The most common arrangement in most nonprofits is to elect officers from among the directors (rather than from a pool of non-directors). This results in the officer leaders coming from a pool of directors who already know the organization and already know the other directors.

If the bylaws specify a range of directors rather than a particular number, the board has the flexibility to bring in new directors as additional skills are needed, rather than to fill an arbitrary number of positions. Therefore, stating a generous range of directors is generally advantageous and can often preclude repeated amendments to the bylaws every time the board is expanded by adding a new director.

Many nonprofit organizations have large boards of directors consisting of a number of prominent citizens and dignitaries whose names give prestige to the organization but who often have no time to actually attend any of the board meetings. Nonprofit organizations should exercise considerable caution before deciding to have very large boards of directors, particularly if many will be of an honorific nature rather than "operational." The reason is that the larger the board, the more difficult, expensive, and time consuming it can be to give those directors notice of board meetings and to get a quorum of directors to attend the meeting.

Indeed, very large boards have many of the problems with slow and cumbersome decision making that can plague organizations with very large voting memberships (as discussed above). An alternative to consider in lieu of a very large board is to create an advisory body, honorary council, or similar structure consisting of prominent individuals or experts on technical issues with non-voting advisory status only. Since such individuals are not true voting directors, they are not counted in determining whether a quorum is present and are not expected to attend board meetings, but instead can be called upon for advice and assistance as needed. Thus, they are able to lend their prominent names and their occasional advice to the organization without bogging down the board's normal decision-making process.

COMPENSATION OF DIRECTORS

Most directors serving on nonprofit boards serve as unpaid volunteers. BoardSource's *Nonprofit Governance Index 2007* showed that only 3 percent of the responding organizations paid a fee or honorarium for board service beyond reimbursement of expenses. Whether or not directors are to be compensated should be stated in the bylaws. (Mere reimbursement for expenses of attending board meetings does not constitute compensation, but receiving a salary or honorarium for performing director duties would qualify as compensation.) While most states do permit nonprofit directors to be compensated, some state laws specifically prohibit loans by a nonprofit corporation to its directors. Other states limit immunity from liability if directors are compensated. While many states allow reasonable compensation of nonprofit directors, compensation is rare in actual practice. Instead, the vast majority of most nonprofit directors donate their time and expertise to the organization as a form of in-kind philanthropy. Accepting no compensation also tends to make directors more unbiased and independent in their oversight, since there is no personal financial gain to affect their decision making.

COMPENSATION IS RARE AND CAN BE LEGALLY RISKY

If a director, officer, or, for that matter, any employee is to be compensated, the law requires that the compensation always be reasonable, which means that total compensation (including any benefits and other perquisites) should be no higher than fair market value as compared to someone with similar education and experience performing similar duties in a similar-size organization. Reasonable compensation can be determined in a number of ways, including by consulting salary surveys or by comparing competitive bids for the same person's services. (However, finding salary surveys covering nonprofit directors would be difficult to do because it is so rare for such directors to be compensated.) Under the so-called intermediate sanctions law set forth in Internal Revenue Code Section 4958, officers and directors are automatically deemed to be "disqualified persons" (meaning that they are deemed to have substantial influence over the organization and therefore must be dealt with at arm's length in any compensation or other financial arrangement they may have with the organization). Consequently, if they receive excessive compensation, it may be possible for the IRS to make them return the excessive amount and pay a penalty tax on the excessive amount. Therefore, it is always prudent to consult legal counsel before paying a salary or other sums to officers and directors of a nonprofit.

METHOD OF SELECTION

Many charities have self-perpetuating boards — boards that determine who shall serve and that may re-elect or reappoint current directors. If an organization has formal voting members, however, most states grant those members the right to select most or all of the board of directors. For instance, one state requires that members with voting rights select at least two-thirds of the directors. Therefore, in organizations with voting members, it is critically important to consult state law because it may mandate how directors are selected and by whom.

Some organizations will designate certain individuals who, because of their position in the organization (or sometimes their position in another organization), automatically serve on the board of directors. These individuals are often referred to as "ex officio." Thus, for example, the bylaws could provide that the chief executive is an ex officio director. There is a common misconception among those serving in nonprofit organizations that the term "ex officio" means that the individual in question has no voting power. However, that is not the meaning of the term (it is a Latin term that essentially means "by virtue of office"). An ex officio director can hold that director position with or without the right to vote. Therefore, an ex officio director's voting or non-voting status should be clearly specified in the bylaws so that there is no confusion on the issue.

TERMS AND LIMITS

Some nonprofits limit the number of consecutive terms an individual may serve. Term limits for directors offer several advantages: They ensure a variety of perspectives by allowing new people to join the board; they help an organization expand its base of contacts in the community; and they prevent inordinate concentration of power among a small group of entrenched leaders. Term limits can also be an easy way for boards to eventually push an underperforming director out the door without having to resort to harsher measures that can cause hard feelings.

However, term limits can also result in the loss of valuable director expertise and institutional memory. Indeed, some organizations find that at about the time that a person becomes very experienced as a director and very knowledgeable about the organization, it is time for that person to step off the board due to term limits. Consequently, organizations with short term limits may find themselves spending inordinate amounts of time constantly training new directors, when that time could be better spent tapping the expertise and experience of those who have served for many years.

Thus, an optimal balance must be struck, weighing the advantages of experience against the benefits of encouraging fresh ideas by inviting new, less experienced people to serve on the board. Some organizations allow particularly valuable directors who have completed the maximum number of terms to return to the board after a one-year sabbatical. The belief is that by making a person sit out just one year before rejoining the board, there is the opportunity for a new person to fill that open board slot (thereby allowing someone with a fresh perspective to join on the board), yet the experienced — and interested — board member is allowed to rejoin relatively quickly so that the board can benefit from that person's prior experience and institutional knowledge.

In BoardSource's *Nonprofit Governance Index 2007,* nearly three-fourths of the respondents reported using three-year terms for directors. Of the organizations that set defined terms of office, the average maximum limit for board service was two terms.

Many nonprofits with relatively large boards have staggered terms for directors, which means that a certain number of directors (but not the entire board) will be chosen in any given year. Staggered terms ensure that there is never a board composed entirely of new directors. Staggered terms can be especially helpful for large boards or boards with short terms of office and in situations where the corporation can benefit from continuity and institutional memory as well as new perspectives. However, staggered terms can be administratively cumbersome to keep track of, and they do require a formal election of some directors to be held every year, which in turn requires a nominating process and other election logistics.

Some nonprofits forego staggered terms and accomplish almost the same thing by simply reelecting a majority of the board each year or every other year (thereby keeping some continuity), while adding a few new directors from time to time to take the place of those who have resigned or no longer desire to serve. Regardless of whether there are staggered terms of office or not, it is a good practice to have the board evaluate the performance of all board members' prior performance before any current director is nominated for re-election.

QUORUM AND VOTING

A quorum is the minimum number of people who must be present to hold a valid membership or board meeting. The quorum may be set by state law or specified in the bylaws. As discussed below, the defined quorum in the bylaws for a directors meeting will normally be higher than the defined quorum for a membership meeting.

In an organization with a large membership spread throughout the country, it is very difficult to get a majority of those members to attend, even if proxies can be mailed in. Therefore, it is normally prudent to set the membership quorum number fairly low. In one state, for example, a nonprofit may in its bylaws establish a quorum as low as one-tenth of the voting membership. The consequence of not providing for a small quorum for annual meetings in the bylaws may be insufficient attendance to constitute a duly authorized meeting or election of directors. The election and any decisions made by directors seated without a quorum may be contested.

Most state laws provide that, in the absence of a contrary provision in the bylaws, a quorum of voting directors (i.e., the number sufficient to hold a valid meeting) is a majority of the voting directors in office. The term "majority" is typically not defined in state law, but it is generally understood to mean anything more than half. Thus, if an entity has a board of 10 people and if only five attend the meeting (either in person or by telephone), there is not a majority in attendance, and, therefore, there is no quorum. (Some nonprofit organizations mistakenly state in their bylaws that a quorum is "a majority of those in attendance." Such a statement makes no sense and is invalid. A quorum must be measured against the total number of voting directors in office.) Usually, state law will limit the minimum percentage of directors in attendance that organizations may select to constitute a quorum; one-third of the directors is often the lowest allowable number.

Although some states allow a quorum of directors to be as low as one-third of the board, careful consideration should be given to whether the board should act without a majority of its directors present. One problem with setting a director quorum below a majority is that it sends the wrong message to the directors that it is not important to come to board meetings. Directors have a duty of care and should always be diligent in keeping themselves informed, and that includes having regular attendance at all board meetings.

Another reason not to set a quorum too low, especially in organizations where all directors do not regularly attend all meetings, is because it can result in a very small portion of the directors taking action that binds the entire organization. For example, if a quorum were set at only one-third of the directors in office, that would mean that only three directors out of a board of nine need attend in order to have a valid meeting; in such a situation, a majority vote would require only two of those three attendees to vote in favor of a matter. Allowing important organizational actions to be decided by two directors out of nine is obviously not prudent operating policy. But even with a board of nine directors where a quorum is defined as a majority, only five directors would need to attend in order to have a valid meeting, and three of the five would have to vote in favor of an action in order for it to pass if the bylaws required a simple "majority of a quorum." Consequently, even with a majority quorum requirement, a relatively small number of directors (three out of nine) can decide matters at a meeting if attendance is low.

For some very important issues, such as the removal of directors or officers, the amendment of the articles of incorporation, the amendment of the bylaws, and decisions to dissolve or merge the corporation, it is common and prudent to require some type of "super-majority voting." This can be accomplished in a number of ways. Perhaps the most common method is to have a provision requiring special actions to be approved by something greater than a simple majority, such as "three-fourths of a quorum of the directors." Another method is to require special actions to be approved by three-fourths of "all the voting directors presently in office." This latter method ensures that important actions cannot be approved too easily at a poorly attended meeting of the directors.

For example, if a board has nine voting directors, a quorum is only five directors, so a bylaws provision requiring "three-fourths of a quorum" results in only *four* directors needing to vote in favor of a matter in order for it to pass. By contrast, requiring "three-fourths of all the directors presently in office," results in *seven* directors needing to vote in favor of the matter in order for it to pass. Thus, depending upon how voting provisions are phrased in the bylaws, it can make a significant difference in how many votes are required for an item to pass.

Another issue that sometimes arises is what happens if a quorum is present at the beginning of a meeting, but some directors subsequently leave early so that there is no quorum later in the meeting. Can votes be taken after a quorum is lost, or must only non-voting matters be discussed from that point forward? The answer is often not clear, and so the best practice is to handle all voting matters very early in the meeting when there clearly is a quorum. But if votes must be taken after a quorum is lost, the first place to look for guidance is legal counsel. However, legal counsel will likely need some advance warning of this issue because he or she will likely have to review both the nonprofit corporation statute and also court cases in the state, which can be very time consuming and cumbersome to research. If state law is silent on the issue, next consult any parliamentary authority that the corporation may have adopted. In the absence of clear state law on point in any of the above authorities, the safest approach is to prohibit any voting to take place once a quorum is lost (especially on controversial or punitive matters such as the removal of a director). However, some nonprofits will allow voting on routine matters to take place after a quorum is lost in the absence of any objection from the remaining directors.

VOTING BY PROXY

An area of great confusion among nonprofit boards is the issue of whether directors can vote by proxy. Because dues-paying members are often allowed to vote by proxy, many directors of nonprofit organizations believe that the same proxy rules apply to them. That is usually not the case. Very few states have laws allowing proxy voting by directors. In the vast majority of states, the general rule is that directors must vote in person (or by telephone) at a meeting. Directors have a fiduciary duty (i.e., a legal duty of care to act in the best interests of the organization), and that fiduciary duty is considered so important and so personal that it cannot be exercised through a proxy or substitute. Instead, the director must carry out his or her duties directly, and that includes participation in voting at board meetings. Thus, in most states, proxy voting by directors is improper, and such a vote can be challenged.

VIRTUAL MEETINGS OF DIRECTORS

Another area of confusion is whether directors can vote by electronic mail and thereby conduct a "virtual meeting." Especially in nonprofits with very large boards, there is often a desire to have directors vote by e-mail rather than go to the trouble of calling a formal board meeting.

In the vast majority of states, there is no provision in the law allowing directors to vote by e-mail. Instead, there must be a lawfully called meeting at which directors vote either in person or by telephone or similar means that allow everyone to hear each other simultaneously. A typical law on this point is that of the District of Columbia, where the statute states that directors may participate in a board meeting "by any means of communication by which all persons participating in the meeting *are able to hear one another.*" Obviously, e-mail is not a method of communication in which directors can "hear one another" at the same time. Consequently, while executive staff may be able to informally poll the directors and get their opinions on an issue by e-mail, there can be no true board vote unless a meeting is called or unless the board votes by unanimous written consent in lieu of a meeting (which is discussed later in this book and which may be transmitted by e-mail in most instances).

It should be noted that while the law in most states has not embraced e-mail board voting, the law in many states does allow dues-paying members to vote by electronic mail. Again, the District of Columbia (which as noted above does not allow voting by e-mail for directors) does allow regular members of a nonprofit to vote by e-mail. The nonprofit statute in the District of Columbia provides that "members who vote by mail, telephone call, telegram, cablegram, electronic mail, or telephone transmission shall be deemed present in person" for purposes of measuring a quorum.

One possible reason why the law does not allow directors to vote by e-mail but does allow regular members to do so is because directors have fiduciary duties that are owed to the corporation, and those duties are deemed to be so important that they should be exercised personally and under circumstances where all directors can hear each other simultaneously and engage in a real-time debate. Another reason may involve the difficulty of verifying who actually sent the e-mail. As technology evolves, it will be interesting to see if state laws also continue to evolve and if nonprofit corporation statutes soften their prohibition on the use of electronic mail voting by directors.

VACANCIES

The issue of vacancies includes the interrelated issues of how vacancies are filled, how much a partial term of office is counted toward limits of board service, and when re-election of the board member or officer is scheduled. If state law permits, it may be desirable to allow the remaining directors to fill vacancies. This practice allows the vacancy to be filled quickly and avoids the expense of a membership vote.

On the other hand, it would not be necessary to fill the vacancy immediately if the number of directors that remain after the vacancy still exceeds the minimum stated in the bylaws. For example, some nonprofits have bylaws that list a range for the size of the board of directors, such as "not fewer than five nor more than 15 directors." If the board had 10 members and a vacancy occurred, it would be possible to leave that vacancy empty until the next board election, since there are still far more than the minimum required number of directors remaining.

Officer vacancy can sometimes present its own special challenges, especially where the officer terms of office do not coincide with board terms of office. In most cases, the best solution is to have the bylaws provide for a special board meeting to be called, at which an interim replacement officer can be selected by the board to serve out the remainder of the term of the vacant officer position.

CONFLICTS OF INTEREST

The IRS likes to see nonprofit entities adopt a conflict-of-interest policy to avoid any unlawful personal benefit to directors and officers. A conflict of interest is generally defined as a situation in which a director or officer has divided loyalty (i.e., loyalty to the nonprofit that is in conflict with loyalty to self, family, or another entity).

Financial conflicts of interest are of the most concern to the IRS. For example, if a nonprofit entity is considering purchasing services from a consulting company, and if that consulting company is owned by a director on the nonprofit's board, then that director has a conflict of interest because the director is essentially "on both sides of the transaction." Specifically, the director has a duty as a board member to act in the best interests of the nonprofit and to help it choose the best company at the lowest possible price. But at the same time, the director has conflicting loyalty to his own consulting company to help it make as much profit as possible and to gain as much new business as possible.

Conflicts of interest are not illegal, and sometimes they are unavoidable. But they do need to be addressed and handled properly. The best way to handle conflicts of this kind is to develop a conflict-of-interest policy for the board and to follow it carefully. The IRS has stated that the purpose of a conflict-of-interest policy is to protect the nonprofit organization's interest when it is contemplating entering into a transaction or arrangement that might benefit the private interest of one or more of its officers or directors. The annual information return (Form 990) filed by most nonprofits also asks whether directors are required to annually disclose interests that could give rise to conflicts and whether the organization regularly and consistently monitors and enforces its policy, so these types of processes should be part of any conflict-of-interest policy.

A conflict-of-interest policy can either be in the bylaws if it is relatively brief, or it can be set forth in a separate document if the policy is lengthy. Probably the more common approach is to include a phrase in the bylaws referencing a standalone conflict-of-interest policy, but put the actual policy in a separate document that can be amended by the board quickly and efficiently without the need to go through the sometimes cumbersome bylaws amendment process. (See Appendix 2 for a sample policy recommended by the IRS that is lengthy enough to be outside of the bylaws.)

At a minimum, it should define in general terms what a conflict is, require disclosure to the full board of any actual or potential conflict by any director, have the board decide (with the help of legal counsel if necessary) if a true conflict of interest exists, and preclude the conflicted director from voting on any transaction in which the director has a conflict. As long as the conflict is disclosed and the conflicted director does not vote on the transaction, the remainder of the board may approve the transaction if it deems it to be in the best interests of the organization. The following example illustrates this principle.

Board member Brenda is one of the best wildlife photographers in the country and has a company called Wildlife Photos, Inc. She sits on the board of The Wildlife Protection Foundation, a nonprofit charity, which desires to hire a photographer to make a wildlife documentary film that is in furtherance of the charity's mission. Brenda is among several photographers asked to respond to a request for proposals. At the board meeting where the various proposals are being analyzed, Brenda discloses to the board in accordance with the charity's conflict-of-interest policy that she is the owner of Wildlife Photos, Inc., and that she therefore has a conflict of interest and should not vote on the various proposals. After answering questions that the board has about her particular proposal, Brenda is asked to leave the room and not participate in the discussion and analysis of the various proposals. The remaining disinterested directors determine, after careful discussion, that Brenda's proposal is by far the best, that the price her company is charging is fair and reasonable and is no higher than fair market value when compared to the other proposals, and that hiring Brenda's company would be in the best interests of the organization. Under these circumstances, the conflict of interest was properly disclosed and properly handled, and the foundation can lawfully hire Brenda.

In short, a good conflict-of-interest policy will provide clear-cut procedures so that a director is not placed in the awkward position of approving a transaction between the nonprofit corporation and himself or herself, or approving a transaction that may provide financial or other benefits to family members or to for-profit organizations owned by the board member or his or her family.

OFFICERS

The officers of an organization are the organization's leaders. They are typically responsible for certain areas of activity and for carrying out the policies of the board. While people often use differing terminology, there are generally two types of officers. The first type is typically referred to as the "board officer," and it is the main focus of this section. As discussed below, board officers are usually unpaid volunteers who are elected to their office by the directors (or by the members in a membership organization). Board officers have fiduciary duties that are owed to the organization pursuant to state law, although in nonprofits with a paid staff, the board officers do not manage the day-to-day operations of the organization. The second type of officer is the staff officer. As noted at the end of this section, staff officers are normally senior employees who are hired and paid by the organization and whose duties involve managing the day-to-day operations of the organization.

Positions of volunteer board officers and their duties are stated in the bylaws. Typically, state law allows nonprofit boards to have any officers with any titles that they desire, but the most common arrangement is to have at least a chair (referred to in some states as a president), a secretary, and a treasurer.

Organizations that seek to groom a person for succession to the chair position will sometimes create the position of vice chair or chair-elect to assist the chair during his or her term; the bylaws would state that the vice chair or chair-elect would automatically move into the chair position at the end of his or her term. Other organizations have either a formal or informal system of grooming people for leadership by having people move up through the officer ranks in sequence (e.g., from secretary to treasurer to chair).

Bylaws typically define the duties of officers, but those definitions should be broad and flexible enough that new duties can be added by the board without the need to amend the bylaws. For example, each officer's duties might include the phrase "and such other duties as the board may assign." In most organizations with a professional staff, the treasurer seldom actually handles or accounts for money but instead reviews financial reports from the staff and interacts with accountants and auditors to help keep the board informed of financial matters. Similarly, an organization with a professional staff will usually handle sending out notices of board meetings and taking minutes at those meetings, which are normally duties of the secretary. In such a case, the secretary is left with only the modest duty of reviewing and editing the final meeting minutes and performing any other duties that the board may assign.

Directors on the board often choose officers from among themselves for annual or multiyear terms. The bylaws should state whether officers must be directors. In other words, it is possible to have someone who is an officer but not a board member. In such instances, the person has no voting power (since voting power belongs only to board members) and merely serves to carry out the wishes of the board. But the more common arrangement (and the preferable arrangement in most instances) is to have officers chosen from the board, in which case such people have both voting power and officer duties.

Some state laws prohibit a person from serving simultaneously in two offices, such as chair and secretary. The reason for this restriction is that the secretary is often required to sign documents attesting to the signature of the chair; thus, two different people are needed. Limitations of this kind, whether required or desired, should be stated in the bylaws. Where permitted, the offices of secretary and treasurer are often combined and held by one person, especially on small boards.

As noted above, board officers are to be distinguished from "staff officers," who are typically salaried full-time employees who manage the organization on a daily basis, such as the chief executive officer, the chief financial officer, and the chief operating officer. These individuals, while having the word "officer" in their titles, are often not specified in the officer section of the bylaws and typically are removed from the job pursuant to the provisions of their employment contract or the organization's personnel policies, rather than pursuant to any provisions in the bylaws.

CHIEF EXECUTIVE

The bylaws may, but are not required to, state the relationship of the chief executive with the board and the responsibilities of the chief executive position. More often, the duties of the chief executive are set forth in a separate job description or possibly in a contract of employment. This salaried professional is typically not a board officer but is responsible to the board of directors. The bylaws should specify whether the chief executive is a director on the board and, if so, whether he or she is a voting director or instead is a director without voting power.

Many chief executives value a seat on the board because it encourages other board members to relate to the executive as a peer rather than a subordinate. On the other hand, the chief executive works for the board and is evaluated (and can be fired) by the board, so in many respects, the chief executive is not a peer to the other directors. If the chief executive is to be made a director, it is more common to make that person a nonvoting director. This allows the chief executive to express opinions and provide nonbinding advice but not be counted toward a quorum and not be able to vote on his or her performance evaluation and compensation. (Of course, the chief executive would also have a conflict of interest when it comes to discussions regarding his or her compensation and performance evaluation, so under any normal conflict-of-interest policy, the chief executive should recuse himself or herself from that portion of a board meeting anyway, even if he or she had voting power.)

EXAMPLE 1

The Clean Energy Advocacy Association is a nonprofit 501(c)(4) social welfare organization. Its bylaws indicate that "the board shall consist of nine at-large voting directors, plus the chief executive, who shall be an ex officio director *without* vote." Because the chief executive is a non-voting director, the chief executive would be invited to board meetings and could participate in discussions with the other directors but would not be counted toward a quorum, would not be allowed to make motions, and would not be allowed to vote. Consequently, for all intents and purposes, the chief executive is an advisor only, despite holding the additional title of "director." If a quorum is defined in the bylaws as a "majority" of the voting directors, then a majority of nine means that five directors must be present to have a meeting. If only four voting directors plus the chief executive attend a meeting, there would not be a quorum.

EXAMPLE 2

Assume the same facts as in Example 1, except that the bylaws state that "the board shall consist of nine at-large voting directors, plus the chief executive, who shall be an ex officio director *with* vote." Because the chief executive is a voting director in this example, the chief executive would be counted toward a quorum, would be allowed to vote, and would be allowed to make motions. Because the chief executive makes the tenth voting director listed in the bylaws, a quorum would be a majority of 10, which means six directors must be present to have a lawful meeting. Thus, there are important quorum and other meeting ramifications that attach to making a chief executive a voting director.

REMOVAL OF DIRECTORS AND OFFICERS

ATTENDANCE

Board service is a major responsibility. A board member must meet the fiduciary duties of careful and prudent judgment, loyalty, adherence to organizational purpose and rules, and avoidance of conflicts of interest. To discharge their fiduciary duties, directors must be able to attend meetings. Deliberation and participation are integral elements of board service.

To encourage attendance, some nonprofit organizations have bylaws provisions that allow the automatic removal of directors who miss a specified number of meetings (either in a year or in a row). Such provisions sometimes contain references to "excused" or "unexcused" absences, although this raises the issue of what will be considered an excused absence, who has the power to excuse that absence, and whether many excused absences are any less detrimental to board decision making than a few unexcused ones. To avoid these issues, some organizations treat all absences the same. Of course, one danger of a strict attendance policy is that it could result in the removal of a good director who has missed several meetings simply because of a period of extended illness. On the other hand, one would hope that a director with an extended serious illness would acknowledge his or her inability to give proper attention to board duties and would voluntarily resign. But if a director with several absences does not take steps to resign, the chair of the board may need to be proactive and politely encourage the director to do so for the good of the organization (as well as to protect the non-participating director from personal liability for dereliction of duty).

Given that state laws normally allow a director to be counted as "present" if the person participates in a meeting by telephone, and given that most people have cell phones that arguably allow them to call into a board meeting from nearly anywhere in the world, there should be little excuse for directors being absent from most board meetings that have been announced sufficiently in advance. Therefore, there is some merit in having some type of reasonable director attendance policy in the bylaws and enforcing it. Alternatively, the bylaws could provide that board meeting attendance will be strongly considered in determining whether a director will be re-elected to another term.

CAUSE

Bylaws often include provisions that describe the removal of officers or directors "with cause" or "without cause." The term "without cause" means literally what it says — the board does not need any reason to remove someone from office. The term "with cause" contemplates some type of misconduct or neglect of duty. However, the term does not have a precise legal meaning, which is why some bylaws will attempt to define in some detail the precise circumstances that constitute "cause."

Removal without cause can help avoid a lawsuit for reinstatement by the person removed, since a court is highly unlikely to reinstate someone as a director when the bylaws allow removal for no reason. Removal without cause also can diminish internal discord regarding the removal and can help avert possible claims of defamation of character (since potentially negative allegations concerning the individual are not necessary).

The inclusion of without-cause language is especially desirable when the officer or board member is also a paid employee, such as the chief executive, since the person essentially cannot dispute the reason for the removal because no reason needs to be stated. If the bylaws indicate that the chief executive can only be removed from office for cause, and if "cause" is defined to include only a very narrow range of misconduct that the organization is not able to prove convincingly with hard evidence, the chief executive could sue and might convince a court to either reinstate the person into office (often with a court also ordering that the nonprofit give back pay for any time the chief executive has been dismissed). Whenever an officer, director, or senior executive is removed for cause and then successfully sues to get reinstated, it causes considerable embarrassment for the organization, not to mention a considerable expenditure of legal fees and time. Therefore, bylaws (and employment contracts) should allow for termination "with or without cause" whenever possible.

Two examples of when to choose the most appropriate means of removal of a nonprofit official and the ramifications of termination with cause are as follows:

EXAMPLE 1

Joe Jones is a director on the board of a nonprofit specialty organization called the Cardiac Physicians Association, which offers educational conferences and useful products to physicians in the field of cardiology. Joe's best friend is Sam, who is a director at a competing organization called the Heart Health Education Foundation. Both organizations compete for the same pool of physician members and both offer educational conferences that appeal to the same cardiologists. However, most cardiologists only have time to attend one conference each year, so the organization that holds the better conference tends to take away attendees from the other organization. Ever since Joe joined the board of the association, his fellow directors have noticed that Sam's competing foundation always seems to get the jump on the association and steal away members and business. Strong circumstantial evidence indicates that board member Joe leaked sensitive and confidential information about the association's strategic plans to Sam. Specifically, within just a few weeks after a board meeting at which Joe's association discussed confidential plans to permanently move its annual educational conference to San Diego and to always hold the conference in June, Sam's competing foundation made a public announcement that it had developed an annual educational conference to be held in San Diego every May. Additionally, the keynote speaker for the first such conference happens to be the same person that Joe's group was contemplating for its June conference. Consequently, there is a high likelihood that cardiologists will attend the May meeting of the foundation and not the June meeting of the association. However, nobody can prove with absolute certainty that Joe was the source of the leak. The bylaws allow directors to be removed "with or without cause." On the above facts, Joe's organization cannot prove with any degree of certainty that there was direct misconduct or a violation of confidentiality by Joe, even though Joe is very likely at fault. Consequently, any removal of Joe from his director position should be done "without cause," which will allow the organization to get rid of this problematic director without having to get into a factual fight over whether there was or was not "cause" for removal.

EXAMPLE 2

Sally Jones is the chief executive of a nonprofit corporation. The bylaws state that the chief executive and other officers can only be removed "for cause," which is narrowly defined in the bylaws as "repeated acts of insubordination or repeated dereliction of duty." Sally was belligerent on the telephone with the president of the organization on one occasion in January, and she also did only minimal work as the chair of the conference planning committee, resulting in a lackluster and poorly attended annual conference that lost money for the first time in the history of the corporation. Sally blames the poor conference on the recent economic recession. During much of the year, she also seemed to be going about her duties without much enthusiasm, although work did get done on time. Under these circumstances, it would be very risky to try to remove Sally "for cause," because there is insufficient evidence of "repeated" acts of insubordination or "repeated" acts of dereliction of duty. If Sally were removed, she might successfully sue to be reinstated. The board should amend the bylaws to allow removal of officers "with or without cause," and the term "cause" should not be narrowly defined to require "repeated" acts, because that kind of language almost always leads to a debate as to how many acts it takes to have "repeated" misconduct. Instead, any definition of "cause" should always include a final catch-all category for "any other activity that is not in the best interests of the corporation, as determined by the board at its sole discretion."

In rare cases, removal without cause can be abused for political purposes, can make a board appear to be acting arbitrarily, and may in extreme cases chill dissenting views or vigorous debate. But a mature board will normally recognize the difference between occasional vigorous — but polite — debate on a controversial issue (which is a healthy and welcome board activity) and a director who constantly complains about everything at every meeting and who verbally attacks other directors without offering any constructive advice (which is an unhealthy board activity warranting removal).

On balance, allowing removal without cause is generally prudent from a legal point of view because it completely avoids any possible legal fight over whether there was or was not sufficient misconduct by a board member to warrant removal. But one option for boards that do not want to allow removal without cause is to simply have short terms of office for board members (such as one-year terms), in which case a director who has been underperforming or who is otherwise problematic can be allowed to serve out the term and then simply not be nominated for re-election.

In some states, a seated director may be removed only for cause. If the removal of an officer or director is contemplated and it is anticipated that the person may challenge such removal, legal counsel should be consulted if possible.

WHO HAS AUTHORITY TO REMOVE?

Many states permit only the body responsible for electing the director to remove the director. Thus, in nonprofits in which directors are selected by voting members or by chapters or regional corporations, a meeting of the members or chapter may have to be called before a director can be removed. Needless to say, removal in such circumstances can be slow and cumbersome. One option that may be possible under state law is to have the removal vote conducted by electronic (e-mail) ballot, which can often be accomplished relatively quickly. But if removal by the membership would be too cumbersome or difficult, probably the best option is the one mentioned above, which is to simply have short terms of office for directors so that a director who is problematic can be allowed to serve out the relatively short term and then simply not be nominated for re-election.

In many nonprofits where there is a problematic director, an informal process that is not part of the bylaws is followed to try to remove the person from office. Typically, the chair of the board would talk privately to the problematic director and try to convince the person to resign voluntarily. Alternatively, or in addition, a group of the most senior and influential board members would meet with the problematic director and ask for his or her voluntary resignation. In most cases, the foregoing is enough to let the director know that further service is not welcomed, and the director will typically resign voluntarily. But if not, then the bylaws must be followed and a special meeting may need to be called at which the appropriate body can meet to vote on removal.

MEETINGS

ANNUAL MEETINGS

Nearly all states require corporations to hold at least an annual meeting. If there are no members, the corporation's annual meeting is a meeting of the board of directors where the prior year is reviewed, the coming year is previewed, and officers and directors are elected. If there are voting members, the annual meeting is typically the one major opportunity for the staff and leadership to meet face-to-face with those dues-paying members and provide them with reports and other information about the activities, finances, and strategic plans of the organization, in addition to the election of directors and officers and the transaction of other business that may be necessary. If permitted by state law, many corporations with large memberships elect directors by mail or e-mail ballot, or they devise a simple proxy form for use by members who will not be able to attend the annual meeting. In many nonprofit membership organizations, the annual meeting is held in conjunction with the annual educational conference to ensure the largest attendance of members possible.

Perhaps the biggest challenge of an annual membership meeting at which voting occurs is ensuring that a quorum of members attend the voting portion of the meeting. While quorum issues are discussed elsewhere in this book (see page 33), it bears repeating that a quorum should not be set too high in the bylaws, especially in organizations where annual membership meetings are lightly attended. The reason is that if too few members attend the meeting to constitute a quorum, then no lawful votes can be taken, which could leave board and officer elections and any planned bylaws amendments in limbo until another meeting can be called at which a quorum can be obtained. Consequently, using mail or electronic balloting (if allowed by state law and the bylaws) is often a safer way to ensure that sufficient voting participation occurs.

In addition to the annual meeting, most nonprofit boards will have additional general meetings during the year on dates that are set and announced well in advance in order for the board to stay apprised of important developments in the organization and properly act as fiduciaries and overseers. While there is no state law requiring any particular number of periodic board meetings, there is at least one charity watchdog organization sponsored by the Better Business Bureau that recommends "at least three evenly spaced meetings per year" of the full governing body with a majority of directors in attendance and with face-to-face participation. Probably the better approach is to have the directors and officers meet as often as necessary to deal with the business at hand and to fulfill their fiduciary duty to keep themselves adequately informed. In a large organization with numerous program activities and complex finances, it may be necessary for a board to meet monthly, whereas a small nonprofit with a modest budget and modest program activities may require less frequent board meetings, although directors may communicate informally on frequent occasions during the year as they carry out the work of the corporation.

SPECIAL MEETINGS

In addition to regular meetings of the board of directors and the members, state laws also allow special meetings to be called. As the name implies, special meetings are typically meetings that are not planned well in advance and that are necessary to deal with some emergency or other special issue that cannot wait until the next scheduled general meeting. The bylaws should specify the number of members necessary to call a special membership meeting and the person who may call special board or executive committee meetings.

State law will often also dictate who can call special board and membership meetings, so it is important to ensure that the bylaws are consistent with state law in this regard. If state law is silent on who can call special meetings, it is common in nonprofit bylaws to have special board meetings called by the chair or by a written request made to the chair by some specified percentage of the directors (such as one-third or more of the directors). Because board meetings can be held by telephone, a demand for a special board meeting is generally not onerous. For special meetings of dues-paying members, and especially in very large membership organizations, it must be kept in mind that such meetings can be quite expensive and time consuming to conduct, so it should be relatively difficult for special membership meetings to be called. If state law is silent on who can call special membership meetings, it is common in nonprofit bylaws to have special meetings of the members called by the chair, by some specified percentage of the directors via a written request to the chair, and/or by some specified percentage of the membership (perhaps 25 percent or more) via a written request to the chair.

NOTICE

It is important to comply precisely with state law regarding notifying members and directors of upcoming meetings. Many states permit nonprofits to choose the notice period by stating it in the bylaws. For example, state law might say that "unless otherwise specified in the bylaws, notice of a board meeting must be given at least twenty days in advance." In the foregoing example, state law would allow the bylaws to specify any longer or shorter period of notice, and only if the bylaws were silent would the state law default of 20 days apply.

Many states provide a range of time for notice of meetings, depending on whether the notice is for a board meeting or a membership meeting. For example, one state's law indicates that notice of a membership meeting is deemed to be reasonable if it is given "not fewer than 10 nor more than 50 days in advance of the meeting." The periods may also vary depending on whether first-class mail is used. For example, one state requires that written notice of meetings be given personally or by first-class mail to each member entitled to vote at the meeting; thus, sending a notice by fax or e-mail does not comply with that law. Some states permit the notice to be included in membership publications sent by bulk mail if they are sent far enough in advance of the meeting. The more modern trend in some states is to allow notice of meetings by e-mail.

The bylaws should allow for notice of a board meeting by any means permitted by state law. E-mail obviously is extremely fast and inexpensive, and, thus, is especially advantageous for giving notice of board meetings when there are large numbers of directors. Providing for an expedient method of notice for special board meetings allows the organization to deal with emergency situations in a timely fashion. For regular board meetings, it is best to plan and announce the dates a year in advance so that busy board members can plan their schedules accordingly.

WAIVER OF NOTICE

Most states allow for waiver of notice. In other words, if notice is required by law and is not given or is improperly given, the meeting may still be held and business may still be conducted if the directors sign a statement that waives notice, or if they attend the meeting without objecting to a lack of notice. A waiver provision is desirable in order to avoid disputes about meeting notice.

Board Action With and Without a Meeting

Most states provide that board action can be taken only at an in-person conference, a teleconference, or any two-way communication medium where all directors can simultaneously hear each other. Consequently, conducting a board meeting or taking a board vote simply by sending out an e-mail and getting back a majority of affirmative responses would not be allowed. This example illustrates this problem.

The board of the Clean Water Foundation desires to remove board member Nathan from office because of repeated failures to attend board meetings. State law and the bylaws both indicate that directors can be removed from office by a majority vote of the board at any meeting called specifically for that purpose. Because the board is very large and its directors are very busy, the chair of the board has decided that it is not practical to call a formal board meeting. Instead, the chair sends an e-mail to all directors containing a resolution that calls for the removal of Nathan. More than a majority of the directors respond to the e-mail message and indicate their approval of Nathan's removal. In the above scenario, Nathan could easily go to court and challenge the validity of his removal. The reason is that removal must take place at a "meeting" called for that purpose, and no meeting was held in this instance. Attempting to remove directors or take other major actions by simply asking a majority of directors to respond to an e-mail is not allowed in most states.

Most states allow board action without a meeting if the bylaws permit it; however, many of these states require that the board action be achieved via "unanimous" consent in writing that is signed by all directors. A unanimous consent form is essentially equivalent to a written ballot, and it will be valid if it is signed and sent in by each director. Because most states require that written consents be unanimous, if even one director accidentally or intentionally fails to submit a written consent (or votes against the matter), the matter being voted on will not be enacted.

Adding unanimous written consent procedures to the bylaws

can be advantageous for quick decision making, and every nonprofit should have this option available in the event a board meeting cannot be called and quick action is needed. Because most states allow electronic signatures, and because most states do not dictate how unanimous consent forms are to be returned to the organization by the directors, it would be permissible in most states for directors to sign a consent form electronically using almost any form of signature and then e-mail the form back to the corporation. Thus, voting by written consent can be a back-door way of allowing directors to vote via e-mail, provided that 100 percent of the directors return their consent forms and vote in favor of the matter at issue.

Some boards may also want to conduct informal meetings and discuss issues by use of e-mail or other nontraditional methods of communication. Most state laws would not allow a formal vote to take place at these types of meetings, but the use of e-mail is otherwise a quick and effective way for directors to stay in touch and conduct the necessary background discussions that may eventually lead to a formal vote at a later, properly called meeting.

COMMITTEES

While the board of directors has the ultimate responsibility for the governance of a nonprofit organization, the board is often assisted by one or more committees. Committees can consist of a subset of the directors or can consist of people who are not directors. Some committees are delegated authority by the board to make certain decisions regarding a particular area of responsibility, while other committees are advisory only. Some nonprofits also form work groups that are less formal than a committee and that may last for only short periods of time to handle some special project. These groups are sometimes referred to as task forces.

Regardless of the name of the committee or task force, it is important that its composition and the scope of its authority be set forth in some document. While many nonprofits list at least the permanent standing committees in their bylaws, some organizations find it more convenient to list all committees in a separate document outside the bylaws, sometimes referred to as administrative regulations. The advantage of putting committee details in such a document is that it can be changed quickly and efficiently by the board of directors. By contrast, putting too much committee detail in the bylaws can sometimes be problematic because changing any part of that committee detail requires a formal bylaws change, which can be an especially slow and cumbersome process in a large membership organization. If committees are to be listed outside of the bylaws, a simple statement in the bylaws can read as follows:

> The board shall have the right to appoint and determine the composition and authority of such standing committees and other committees and task forces as it deems necessary from time to time. Such committees and task forces may be described in separate administrative regulations or in resolutions of the board.

Again, it is important to consult state law when drafting bylaws provisions involving committees. In some states, a committee that has any portion of the powers of the board must consist of all board members. (For example, an executive committee normally has the power of the board between meetings and should be composed of some subset of the directors.) But a committee that does not exercise any power and that has only advisory authority can normally consist of non-directors. (For example, a government relations committee that makes nonbinding recommendations to the board on a lobbying strategy for the organization could consist of some or all non-directors with legislative expertise.) In some nonprofits, committees have their own "charter" or similar document indicating in some detail the authority, composition, and other features of each committee that are too numerous to put into bylaws. Such committee charters are typically approved by the board but are kept separate from the bylaws.

EXECUTIVE COMMITTEE

Boards should always have a serious discussion before deciding to form any type of committee, since excessive committee structures can unnecessarily complicate governance and splinter decision-making authority. One committee that may be worth consideration for organizations with large boards that meet infrequently is an executive committee, which could act on behalf of the board between meetings. Executive committees are usually — and in some states are required to be — composed exclusively of directors; this is because the executive committee exercises nearly all of the authority of the board.

The advantage of an executive committee is that it enables a large, geographically scattered board to function with dispatch in between regular meetings of the board. The danger is that the existence of an aggressive executive committee may encourage the full board to relax its sense of commitment and accountability. On balance, however, most nonprofits are well served to have an executive committee unless the board of directors consists of a small enough number of people that the full board can always act quickly and efficiently.

If an executive committee is authorized, the bylaws should identify its composition. The bylaws can also specify how much notice is needed for its meetings and who may convene the meeting, but care should be taken to avoid limiting the committee's ability to act promptly. And if there are any desired limitations on the authority of the executive committee, those limitations should be stated in the bylaws as well.

State law seldom regulates the procedures of an executive committee; however, the law often limits or denies the committee authority to act in certain situations. In many states, a committee of the board, as opposed to the full board, does not have the authority to

- approve a dissolution, merger, or sale of all the corporation's assets

- appoint or remove directors

- amend the bylaws or the articles of incorporation

STANDING COMMITTEES

If the board deems it necessary and appropriate, the bylaws may include a provision for the board to form one or more standing committees, which are permanent committees of the organization (as opposed to temporary task forces that can be formed and disbanded as the need arises). Some organizations list their standing committees in the bylaws. Others, wanting more flexibility, don't name standing committees and simply state the board's right to establish such committees as needed. Charges for such committees can then be established by board resolutions.

Among the most common standing committees are the executive committee, finance committee, audit committee, and governance committee. (In some organizations, the governance committee may go by various names and may be responsible for board development, nominations, and/or the development of bylaws amendments.)

The bylaws should allow a board to appoint some committee members from outside the board, a practice that enables people with expertise, which the board itself may lack, to be included on key committees. This can be especially useful for the finance or audit committees. However, it must also be kept in mind that non-board members serving on a committee normally do not owe any fiduciary duties to the organization, such as the duty of confidentiality. Consequently, nonprofits must proceed with caution when sharing sensitive financial or strategic information with such outsiders.

STANDARDS OF CONDUCT AND CODES OF ETHICS

Officers and directors have a fiduciary relationship to the nonprofit. This means they must act in the best interest of the organization. These fiduciary duties are sometimes specified in the state corporation act or are developed over time in court decisions.

Nonprofit policies (and sometimes bylaws) may also refer to expectations for the ethical conduct of officers and directors and, less frequently, to expectations for other volunteers serving the organization. Expectations of conduct for paid staff are normally dealt with in the organization's personnel manual. Some organizations have adopted a "statement of fiduciary responsibility," which is external to the bylaws and explains these standards of conduct. If the nonprofit has adopted standards of conduct, such as a code of ethics or disciplinary code governing its board or members, the bylaws often authorize the adoption and revision of such standards by the board. In addition, some nonprofits include in their policies or bylaws a statement of nondiscrimination in carrying out their activities.

While having directors adopt a code of ethics or statement of nondiscrimination is common and can help to memorialize the organization's desire to adhere to high standards, it must be remembered that federal and state laws prohibit discrimination and certain kinds of unethical conduct regardless of whether the organization has a code of ethics or not. Therefore, having directors sign a nondiscrimination statement is to some degree "window dressing" because they are not allowed by law to discriminate on many grounds even without signing such a statement.

FINANCIAL CONTROLS

The bylaws may provide for financial controls, such as

- a clause allowing for officer or employee "bonding" (i.e., a guarantee by an outside party, usually an insurance company, to reimburse the organization for losses incurred as a result of an employee's theft, negligence, or fraud)

- a clause covering who has check-signing authority (i.e., who is authorized to write checks and up to what amount without board approval)

- a clause mandating an annual audit to be reviewed by the audit committee and the full board

- a clause requiring financial statements to be prepared by a qualified party and reviewed by the finance committee and full board

More often, however, such provisions and procedures are in separate policy statements so that the bylaws do not become unnecessarily cluttered with excessive detail. Accountants and auditors for the organization are probably in the best position to assist in ensuring that financial controls are adequate and are sufficiently documented.

INDEMNIFICATION, IMMUNITY, AND INSURANCE

Most states have adopted laws offering or authorizing some protection for volunteers in defending against litigation connected to their service to a nonprofit. These volunteer protection laws permit or mandate corporate indemnification (discussed in more detail below) and provide some level of immunity.

INDEMNIFICATION

Indemnification is the payment or reimbursement by the nonprofit to an affected individual (board member, officer, employee, volunteer) for legal expenses, such as judgments, some costs, and attorney fees, incurred as a result of service to the nonprofit. Many states allow indemnification to extend to activities carried out on behalf of the organization, such as service on an affiliate organization's board of directors, in addition to those carried out directly for the organization, such as participation on the board of directors.

Some states require a provision to be contained in the bylaws to implement the allowed indemnification. In drafting such a provision, a nonprofit may wish to include limitations on indemnification, and many states limit the circumstances in which indemnification may be granted. Generally, indemnification cannot be offered when a board member breaches his or her fiduciary duty, acts in bad faith, or commits criminal misconduct. A bylaws section authorizing the nonprofit to indemnify individuals, subject to any limitations identified, should be included in every nonprofit's bylaws. Such an indemnification provision encourages capable people to serve on the board.

Where state law permits indemnification, insurance may be available, subject to limitations in the policy (discussed below). Insurance can be a very important protection against liability. Indemnification has little value if the organization has no or few assets. For substantial organizations, insurance can help protect their assets.

INSURANCE

Nonprofit organizations may wish to include a provision in their bylaws authorizing the nonprofit to purchase directors' and officers' (D&O) liability insurance. Such a provision encourages directors to address the issue of insurance. While insurance policies offer some protection, it is very important that directors know the coverage and limitations of the D&O and other insurance policies covering them and the property of the nonprofit.

Many nonprofit organizations purchase D&O liability insurance policies, and then their officers and directors assume they need not worry any more about personal liability. But it is usually foolhardy to assume that an insurance policy will cover every conceivable situation. Indeed, D&O insurance policies should be carefully reviewed, preferably by legal counsel, because such policies often do contain a number of exceptions for situations not covered by the policy, such as lawsuits alleging defamation, sexual assault, or other types of misconduct. Thus, even with insurance, directors and officers may be at some risk, although it would usually be in cases of intentional and knowingly criminal or other very serious misconduct. If there are exceptions, it may be possible to purchase an extra "rider" or supplemental policy to fill in at least some of the exceptions in the main D&O policy.

AMENDMENT OF BYLAWS

The need for bylaws amendments can arise in a number of ways. For example, the law can change. Additionally, an organization can change as it expands its programs and matures over time such that initial bylaws provisions that seemed appropriate when the organization was formed have now become outdated. Societal norms and customs may also change. And sometimes, if initial bylaws were drafted by inexperienced people or were created in a hurry, those bylaws may not have adequately covered all pertinent voting procedures and other governance issues that the organization may face. Since an organization is obligated to operate within the limitations of its bylaws, it simply cannot ignore bylaws provisions that are inconvenient, incomplete, or outdated. If a bylaws provision no longer fits the organization's current situation or preferred method of operation, the bylaws provision must be formally changed.

Consequently, it is prudent to have a committee or legal counsel review the bylaws periodically (perhaps every other year) to ensure that the bylaws still reflect standard practice within the organization and to ensure that there have been no changes to state laws or other nonprofit requirements that would affect the bylaws. In addition, the bylaws should be reviewed whenever any governance problems arise that are not adequately covered by the existing provisions of the bylaws.

The Form 990 information return should also be carefully reviewed, since it may spur some changes to the bylaws or, more likely, to related policy documents that may be outside of the bylaws. For example, the latest Form 990 now contains a section with several questions about governance policies, such as whether there is a conflict-of-interest policy, a whistleblower policy, a document retention and destruction policy, an executive compensation policy, and a joint venture policy. The Form 990 also asks whether any significant changes were made to any organizational documents, which would include amendments to the bylaws. If so, significant bylaws changes must be described in a schedule to Form 990.

If changes are to be made, it is important to have a well-written clause in the bylaws that details exactly how they can be changed, including whether amendments can be made by the board or by dues-paying members, how changes are developed and reviewed, whether changes can be approved only at a meeting or whether some type of mail ballot to the members is permitted, and what the required vote will be for an amendment to be approved. If there is no clause in the bylaws specifying how the bylaws are to be amended, then organizations may have to refer to their own state's default provisions, which would then control how the bylaws are amended. Those default provisions may not be convenient or appropriate for some organizations. For minor or cosmetic changes to the bylaws, it may be possible even in a membership organization for the bylaws to reserve such changes to the board to speed up the amendment process.

Because bylaws are such important documents, a nonprofit may wish to require the affirmative approval of a greater-than-majority ("supermajority") vote, such as two-thirds or three-fourths of a quorum of those able to vote, to approve amendments to the bylaws. Requiring super-majority voting is especially common where bylaws are approved only by the board of directors because it helps prevent the bylaws from being amended hastily or by a small minority of the voting body. However, in large membership organizations where attendance at meetings may be low or where responses to even e-mail ballots may be very spotty, it may be necessary to set a much more modest approval percentage in order to ensure that bylaws amendments will pass.

Many states require the meeting notice to describe the nature of a proposed amendment. This requirement should be included in the bylaws to help ensure that the proper procedure is followed.

CASE STUDY

The Disability Advocacy Association, a nonprofit organization, currently has a board of nine directors, which is the fixed number specified in the bylaws. The organization is always short of money and struggling to make ends meet. At a meeting of the board, the chair proposes that the board be expanded in size over the next few years, with the primary criteria being that new candidates be prominent people of wealth who will be likely to contribute regularly to the organization and perhaps encourage their friends to do so as well. The other board members agree. As each new candidate for the board is identified by a nominating committee, an e-mail message is sent to the entire board asking for their approval of the new candidate and also asking the board to approve a simultaneous bylaws change increasing the size of the board by one additional position. This process continues over the next few months until two new board members are approved by e-mail, resulting in a total board of 11 and in two consecutive bylaws amendments increasing the size of the board each time.

Because the board members are very prominent and busy politicians and business people, the vast majority are not able to attend any board meetings. The bylaws state that a quorum is a majority of directors. At an annual board meeting scheduled for December 1, three directors attend in person, one director joins the meeting by telephone, and both of the two new directors give their proxy to the chair of the board and tell the chair how they want their votes cast on the various items on the agenda. All other directors are absent. The chair believes that there is a quorum consisting of six out of eleven (with the six allegedly consisting of three in person, one by phone, and the two proxies).

One agenda item is the removal for cause of the organization's chief executive, who is a paid employee and also listed in the bylaws as an "ex officio" officer and director. The bylaws state that officers can only be removed "for cause" by a two-thirds vote of a quorum of the board. The organization has very little evidence of misconduct or dereliction of duty by the chief executive, other than one late report and some anecdotal evidence of sloppy management. When the removal of the chief executive comes up for a vote, the three directors in attendance and the director on the telephone all vote in favor of removal. The two directors who gave their proxy to the chair also asked the chair to cast votes in favor of removal. The chair therefore announces that the vote for removal is a unanimous vote of a quorum.

Bylaws and Other Legal Problems

The association has a host of bylaws problems and other legal problems on its hands. First, the chair has attempted to have the board vote on the addition of new directors and vote on amendments to the bylaws by e-mail, rather than calling a lawful board meeting. In nearly every state, directors cannot vote by e-mail, and such a vote can be challenged.

Consequently, there is considerable doubt that the two new directors really are lawfully elected in the first place or that any of the bylaws amendments were lawfully made. Consequently, the true "board" may still consist of only nine directors. Another problem is that at the December meeting, two directors who could not attend attempted to leave their "proxy" vote with the chair. Again, in nearly every state, directors are not allowed to vote by proxy and such persons cannot be counted toward a quorum. Voting by telephone, however, is allowed and is considered as being present for the meeting. Consequently, the organization only has four directors present at the meeting (three in person and one by phone), so there is no quorum either under the original board of nine or under the possible new board of 11. Moreover, the evidence of wrongdoing that the board has against its chief executive is quite weak, so the chief executive could hire legal counsel and challenge his removal not only because of a lack of a quorum but also because of a lack of clear evidence that there was "cause."

SOLUTIONS AND LESSONS LEARNED

A board should never add directors solely because the people are prominent and wealthy, especially if there is no realistic chance they will attend board meetings. Doing so almost always leads to quorum problems, not to mention adding no meaningful value to the talent on the board. Second, the organization should have amended its bylaws to allow a "range" of directors (such as not fewer than five nor more than 15) so that if new directors are lawfully added over time, there is no need to amend the bylaws each time. The election of new directors and the amendments to the bylaws should always be done at a lawfully called meeting attended by directors in person or by telephone, rather than by e-mail. Electronic meetings are not allowed in most states. To make matters worse, the bylaws merely indicate that the chief executive is "ex officio," but the bylaws do not specify whether the chief executive has voting power or not. The term "ex officio" should always be clarified in the bylaws so that the board knows whether the person is "without vote" or "with vote." The bylaws also only allow removal of the chief executive "for cause." The better and more flexible approach is to have bylaws that allow removal "with or without cause." On relatively weak facts like these, it is always safer to remove a person "without cause" so that the person has no specific allegations to challenge. Finally, board members should never be allowed to leave their "proxy" with the chair, since proxy voting is not allowed in the vast majority of states. If a director cannot attend in person, then every effort should be made to have the person call into the meeting by telephone, which is a form of "attendance" and would count the person toward a quorum.

CONCLUSION

The development of bylaws is sometimes viewed as a technical ordeal with no practical result. To ensure effectiveness, good bylaws must be well written; boards should spend the time and effort required to ensure they comply with state law and the articles of incorporation so that actions of the organization are legally defensible. At the same time, to be useful, bylaws should also provide a clearly written, consistent statement of rules that the board can understand and that are reasonable to implement; they should not be full of complex "legalese" that is difficult to understand or contain unnecessarily harsh or restrictive provisions. Very rarely can inexperienced directors develop coherent, well-organized and effective bylaws that comply with state law and that help organizations avoid common governance pitfalls without having the help of qualified legal counsel. Even experienced directors and nonprofit executives can benefit from having legal review of bylaws periodically as part of an overall "legal audit" of the organization.

Effective nonprofit programs and fundraising depend on policy development and oversight tied not only to the organization's mission and operations but also to its governance. Bylaws that reflect the culture and expectations of the organization and that are carefully considered and implemented can be a powerful tool in this effort.

Governance issues often arise when an organization is growing or contracting or when it faces significant changes in the external environment, such as reduced government or private funding, changes in tax laws, or a difficult economic environment. In such circumstances, how decisions are made has a great effect on the acceptance of those decisions and the overall support and stability of a nonprofit. Bylaws that are not consistent with the culture or current needs of an organization can be a source of discord; in extreme situations, they can severely weaken an organization and even lead to its ultimate dissolution.

Bylaws that are viewed by the nonprofit community as fairly written and administered are valuable resources, capable of promoting sound decisions whatever the circumstances may be. In addition, as one part of a coordinated approach including a strategic plan, oversight of operations, continuous assessment of opportunities and challenges, and the range of talents of directors, the bylaws contribute to the long-term institutional strength of the nonprofit.

The bylaws should be a living document — to be used, reviewed, and revised as necessary. The original bylaws should be drafted in clear terms, and the drafters should carefully consider their decisions concerning procedures and provisions. The organization should provide for regular bylaws review, by a bylaws task force or by legal counsel, to make recommendations to the full board concerning revisions.

In developing bylaws, a nonprofit should not rely solely on forms or provisions that have worked for other groups in different times or with different cultures, expectations, and requirements. Each organization must develop its own bylaws, harmonizing them with its own resolutions, policies, and procedural rules as part of an overall organizational strategy.

Finally, although bylaws are not normally required to be made public, many nonprofit organizations are proud of the well-drafted governance policies and procedures in their bylaws and publish the bylaws as part of an annual report to donors and other members.

APPENDIX 1

SAMPLE ARTICLES OF INCORPORATION

Many states have a sample template for articles of incorporation that is available on the state's Web site. However, that template contains only the minimum language required by state law, and it will almost never contain special federal tax exemption language that is sometimes required by the Internal Revenue Code in order to obtain IRS recognition of tax exemption. Therefore, these templates must be used with caution and are almost never sufficient by themselves to qualify an organization for federal tax exemption.

Set forth below is the main content of one possible set of articles of incorporation for a section 501(c)(3) charity. However, format and content of incorporation laws vary widely from state to state, and depending on the mission of the nonprofit, additional language may be necessary to satisfy the Internal Revenue Service. Therefore, it is foolhardy to file articles of incorporation without first seeking the drafting advice of competent legal counsel.

ARTICLES OF INCORPORATION

THE UNDERSIGNED, who are all natural persons of the age of eighteen years or more, acting as incorporators of a corporation pursuant to the [name of state] Nonprofit Corporation Act, hereby certify:

FIRST: The name of the Corporation is: [insert name] (hereinafter "the Corporation").

SECOND: The period of duration of the Corporation is perpetual.

THIRD: The Corporation is organized and shall be operated exclusively for charitable and educational purposes within the meaning of Section 501(c)(3) of the Internal Revenue Code of 1986, as now in effect or as may hereafter be amended ("the Code"). The specific purposes for which the Corporation is formed include, but are not limited to [inserted more detailed purposes].

FOURTH: The Corporation shall have members. The membership categories and their voting rights shall be as set forth in the bylaws.

FIFTH: The Corporation shall be governed by a board of directors. There shall at all times be at least three directors, who shall be elected or appointed as provided by the Bylaws. The number of directors constituting the initial Board of Directors is XX, and the names and addresses, including street and number of the persons who are to serve as the initial directors until the first annual meeting or until their successors are elected and qualify are as follows: [insert names and addresses]

SIXTH: Provisions for the regulation of the internal affairs of the Corporation, including provisions for distribution of assets on dissolution or final liquidation are as follows:

A. No part of the net earnings of the Corporation shall inure to the benefit of, or be distributable to any director or officer of the Corporation, or any other private person, except that the Corporation shall be authorized and empowered to pay reasonable compensation for services rendered to or for the Corporation and to make payments and distributions in furtherance of the purposes set forth in Article Third hereof.

B. No substantial part of the activities of the Corporation shall be the carrying on of propaganda or otherwise attempting to influence legislation (except as otherwise permitted by Section 501(h) of the Code), and the Corporation shall not participate in, or intervene in (including the publishing or distribution of statements concerning) any political campaign on behalf of (or in opposition to) any candidate for public office.

C. Notwithstanding any other provisions of these Articles, the Corporation shall not directly or indirectly carry on any activity which would prevent it from obtaining exemption from Federal income taxation as a corporation described in Section 501(c)(3) of the Code, or cause it to lose such exempt status, or carry on any activity not permitted to be carried on by a corporation, contributions to which are deductible under Section 170(c)(2) of the Code.

D. In the event of dissolution or final liquidation of the Corporation, all of the remaining assets and property of the Corporation shall, after paying or making provision for the payment of all of the liabilities and obligations of the Corporation and for necessary expenses thereof, be distributed by the Board of Directors for one or more exempt purposes within the meaning of section 501(c)(3) of the Code, or shall be distributed to the federal government, or to a state or local government, for public purposes. In no event shall any of such assets or property be distributed to any director or officer, or to any private individual.

SEVENTH: The address, including street and number, of the initial registered office of the Corporation is [insert address] and the name of its initial registered agent at such address is [insert name].

EIGHTH: The name and address, including street and number, of the incorporators are as follows: [insert names and addresses]

IN WITNESS WHEREOF, the undersigned subscribe these Articles of Incorporation this ____ day of _____, 20XX.

APPENDIX 2

SAMPLE CONFLICT-OF-INTEREST POLICY

The Internal Revenue Service has issued a model conflict-of-interest policy for tax-exempt hospitals, and it often recommends that other types of charitable organizations adopt the same policy with appropriate modifications. The model conflict-of-interest policy is the only suggested policy that the IRS has issued to date.

Outlined below is the IRS's recommended policy with modifications to make it applicable to any nonprofit entity. The policy is also contained as an exhibit to the instructions to Form 1023 (Application for Recognition of Exemption), which can be found at: www.irs.gov/instructions/i1023/ar03.html

Note that this policy is more restrictive than required by many state "interested director" statutes. (It would, for example, preclude an organization from engaging in a transaction with a board member, unless the board cannot find a more advantageous transaction.)

The following template policy from the IRS is offered as an example to provide guidance. It is advisable to consult with counsel prior to adopting a conflict-of-interest policy or any other corporate policy.

[NAME OF CORPORATION]

CONFLICT-OF-INTEREST POLICY

ARTICLE I
Purpose

The purpose of the conflict-of-interest policy is to protect the Corporation's interest when it is contemplating entering into a transaction or arrangement that might benefit the private interest of an officer or director of the Corporation. This policy is intended to supplement but not replace any applicable state laws governing conflicts of interest applicable to nonprofit and charitable corporations.

ARTICLE II
Definitions

1. Interested Person
   Any director, principal officer, or member of a committee with board delegated powers who has a direct or indirect financial interest, as defined below, is an interested person. If a person is an interested person with respect to any entity in the system of which the Corporation is a part, he or she is an interested person with respect to all entities in the system.

2. Financial Interest
   A person has a financial interest if the person has, directly or indirectly, through business, investment or family

   a. an ownership or investment interest in any entity with which the Corporation has a transaction or arrangement, or

   b. a compensation arrangement with the Corporation or with any entity or individual with which the Corporation has a transaction or arrangement, or

   c. a potential ownership or investment interest in, or compensation arrangement with, any entity or individual with which the Corporation is negotiating a transaction or arrangement.

Compensation includes direct and indirect remuneration, as well as gifts or favors that are substantial in nature.

A financial interest is not necessarily a conflict of interest. Under Article III, Section 2, a person who has a financial interest may have a conflict of interest only if the appropriate board or committee decides that a conflict of interest exists.

ARTICLE III

Procedures

1. Duty to Disclose
   In connection with any actual or possible conflicts of interest, an interested person must disclose the existence of his or her financial interest and must be given the opportunity to disclose all material facts to the directors and members of committees with board-delegated powers considering the proposed transaction or arrangement.

2. Determining Whether a Conflict of Interest Exists
   After disclosure of the financial interest and all material facts, and after any discussion with the interested person, he/she shall leave the board or committee meeting while the determination of a conflict of interest is discussed and voted upon. The remaining board or committee members shall decide if a conflict of interest exists.

3. Procedures for Addressing the Conflict of Interest

   a. An interested person may make a presentation at the board or committee meeting, but after such presentation, he/she shall leave the meeting during the discussion of, and the vote on, the transaction or arrangement that results in the conflict of interest.

   b. The chairperson of the board or committee shall, if appropriate, appoint a disinterested person or committee to investigate alternatives to the proposed transaction or arrangement.

c. After exercising due diligence, the board or committee shall determine whether the Corporation can obtain a more advantageous transaction or arrangement with reasonable efforts from a person or entity that would not give rise to a conflict of interest.

d. If a more advantageous transaction or arrangement is not reasonably attainable under circumstances that would not give rise to a conflict of interest, the board or committee shall determine by a majority vote of the disinterested directors whether the transaction or arrangement is in the Corporation's best interest and for its own benefit and whether the transaction is fair and reasonable to the Corporation and shall make its decision as to whether to enter into the transaction or arrangement in conformity with such determination.

4. Violations of the Conflict-of-Interest Policy

a. If the board or committee has reasonable cause to believe that a member has failed to disclose actual or possible conflicts of interest, it shall inform the member of the basis for such belief and afford the member an opportunity to explain the alleged failure to disclose.

b. If, after hearing the response of the member and making such further investigation as may be warranted in the circumstances, the board or committee determines that the member has in fact failed to disclose an actual or possible conflict of interest, it shall take appropriate disciplinary and corrective action.

Article IV

Records of Proceedings

The minutes of the board and all committee with board delegated powers shall contain:

1. The names of the persons who disclosed or otherwise were found to have a financial interest in connection with an actual or possible conflict of interest, the nature of the financial interest, any action taken to determine whether a

conflict of interest was present, and the board's or committee's decision as to whether a conflict of interest in fact existed.

2. The names of the persons who were present for discussions and votes relating to the transaction or arrangement, the content of the discussion, including any alternatives to the proposed transaction or arrangement, and a record of any votes taken in connection therewith.

ARTICLE V

Compensation

1. A voting member of the board of directors who receives compensation, directly or indirectly, from the Corporation for services is precluded from voting on matters pertaining to that member's compensation.

2. A voting member of any committee whose jurisdiction includes compensation matters and who receives compensation, directly or indirectly, from the Corporation for services is precluded from voting on matters pertaining to that member's compensation.

ARTICLE VI

Annual Statements

Each director, principal officer, and member of a committee with board delegated powers shall annually sign a statement which affirms that such person:

a. has received a copy of the conflict-of-interest policy,

b. has read and understands the policy,

c. has agreed to comply with the policy, and

d. understands that the Corporation is a charitable organization and that in order to maintain its federal tax exemption it must engage primarily in activities which accomplish one or more of its tax-exempt purposes.

Article VII
Periodic Reviews

To ensure that the Corporation operates in a manner consistent with its charitable purposes and that it does not engage in activities that could jeopardize its status as an organization exempt from federal income tax, periodic reviews shall be conducted. The periodic reviews shall, at a minimum, include the following subjects:

    a. whether compensation arrangements and benefits are reasonable and are the result of arm's length bargaining.

    b. whether acquisitions of assets or property from any officer or director result in inurement or impermissible private benefit.

Article VIII
Use of Outside Experts

In conducting the periodic reviews provided for in Article VII, the Corporation may, but need not, use outside advisors. If outside experts are used, their use shall not relieve the board of its responsibility for ensuring that periodic reviews are conducted.

APPENDIX 3

SAMPLE WHISTLEBLOWER PROTECTION POLICY

IRS Form 990 has a section asking whether nonprofits have various types of governance policies, including a whistleblower policy. While federal law generally prohibits retaliation against employees for reporting financial wrongdoing or other illegal activity within an organization, the law does not specifically mandate that this be memorialized in a whistleblower policy. Nevertheless, it is considered good governance practice to have such a policy and to ensure that staff and board members are familiar with the policy. A whistleblower policy would almost never be found in the bylaws but would instead typically be either a free-standing document or part of the organization's personnel policy manual. The sample below is just one of many possible ways to draft a whistleblower policy.

WHISTLEBLOWER PROTECTION POLICY

In keeping with the policy of maintaining the highest standards of conduct and ethics, XYZ will investigate any suspected fraudulent or dishonest use or misuse of XYZ's resources or property by staff, board members, consultants, or volunteers.

Staff, board members, consultants, and volunteers are encouraged to report suspected fraudulent or dishonest conduct (i.e., to act as "whistleblower"), pursuant to the procedures set forth below.

REPORTING

A person's concerns about possible fraudulent or dishonest use or misuse of resources or property should be reported to his or her supervisor or, if suspected by a volunteer or consultant, to the staff member supporting the volunteer's or consultant's work. If, for any reason, a person finds it difficult to report his or her concerns to a supervisor or staff member supporting the volunteer's or consultant's work, the person may report the concerns directly to the chief executive. Alternately, to facilitate reporting of suspected violations where the reporter wishes to remain anonymous, a written statement may be submitted to one of the individuals listed above.

DEFINITIONS

Baseless Allegations

Allegations made with reckless disregard for their truth or falsity or allegations that were made maliciously or not in good faith. Individuals making such allegations may be subject to disciplinary action by XYZ and/or legal claims by individuals accused of such conduct.

Fraudulent or Dishonest Conduct

A deliberate act or failure to act with the intention of obtaining an unauthorized benefit.

A non-exhaustive list of examples of such conduct include the following:

- Forgery or alteration of documents

- Unauthorized alteration or manipulation of computer files

- Pursuit of a benefit or advantage in violation of XYZ's conflict-of-interest policy

- Misappropriation or misuse of XYZ resources, such as funds, supplies, or other assets

- Authorizing or receiving compensation for goods not received or services not performed, or paying for services or goods that are not rendered or delivered

- Authorizing or receiving compensation for hours not worked

- Supplying false or misleading information on XYZ's financial or other public documents, including its Form 990 (Annual Information Return)

- Providing false information to or withholding material information from XYZ's board or auditors

- Destroying, altering, mutilating, concealing, covering up, falsifying, or making a false entry in any records that may be connected to an official proceeding, in violation of federal or state law or regulations or otherwise obstructing, influencing, or impeding any official proceeding, in violation of federal or state law or regulations

- Embezzling, self-dealing, or otherwise obtaining an unlawful private benefit (i.e., XYZ assets being used by anyone in the organization improperly for personal gain).

Whistleblower

An employee, consultant, or volunteer who informs a supervisor or the chief executive about an activity relating to XYZ which that person believes to be fraudulent or dishonest.

RESPONSIBILITIES AND INVESTIGATIONS

Supervisors

Supervisors are required to report suspected fraudulent or dishonest conduct to the chief executive. Reasonable care should be taken in dealing with suspected misconduct to avoid

- Baseless allegations

- Premature notice to persons suspected of misconduct and/or disclosure of suspected misconduct to others not involved with the investigation

- Violations of a person's rights under law

Due to the important yet sensitive nature of the suspected violations, effective professional follow-up is critical. Supervisors should not perform any investigative or other follow-up steps on their own. Accordingly, a supervisor who becomes aware of suspected misconduct should report it to the chief executive, but should *not* without prior permission take steps on his or her own to do any of the following:

- Contact the person suspected to further investigate the matter or demand restitution

- Discuss the case with attorneys, the media, or anyone other than the chief executive

- Report the case to an authorized law enforcement officer without first discussing the case with the chief executive

Investigation

All relevant matters, including suspected but unproved matters, will be reviewed and analyzed by an appropriate person designated by the president or executive committee. This may include an investigation by legal counsel and/or accountants in some instances. All investigations will be kept confidential. Appropriate corrective action will be taken, if necessary, and findings will be communicated to the reporting person and his or her supervisor.

WHISTLEBLOWER PROTECTION

- XYZ will use its best efforts to protect whistleblowers against retaliation. Whistleblowing complaints will be handled with sensitivity, discretion, and confidentiality to the extent allowed by the circumstances and the law. Generally, this means that whistleblower complaints will only be shared with those who have a need to know so that XYZ can conduct an effective investigation, determine what action to take based on the results of any such investigation, and in appropriate cases, with law enforcement personnel. (Should disciplinary or legal action be taken against a person or persons as a result of a whistleblower complaint, such persons may also have the right to know the identity of the whistleblower.)

- Employees, consultants, and volunteers of XYZ may not retaliate against a whistleblower for informing management about an activity which that person believes in good faith to be fraudulent or dishonest with the intent or effect of adversely affecting the terms or conditions of the whistleblower's employment, including but not limited to, threats of physical harm, loss of job, punitive work assignments, or impact on salary or fees. Whistleblowers who believe that they have been retaliated against may file a written complaint with the chief executive. Any complaint of retaliation will be promptly investigated and appropriate corrective measures taken if allegations of retaliation are substantiated. This protection from retaliation is not intended to prohibit supervisors from taking action, including disciplinary action, in the usual scope of their duties and based on valid performance-related factors.

- Whistleblowers must be cautious to avoid baseless allegations (as described earlier in the definitions section of this policy). Allegations that are baseless and not made in good faith may result in disciplinary action.

APPENDIX 4

SAMPLE RECORD RETENTION AND DOCUMENT DESTRUCTION POLICY

IRS Form 990 has a section asking whether nonprofits have various types of governance policies, including a document retention and destruction policy. While federal law generally prohibits organizations from altering, covering up, falsifying, or destroying documents in the face of a pending or ongoing government investigation, the law does not specifically mandate that this be memorialized in a written policy. Nevertheless, it is considered good governance practice to have such a policy and to ensure that staff and board members are familiar with the policy. A document retention policy would almost never be found in the bylaws but would instead typically be either a free-standing document or part of the organization's personnel policy manual. The sample below is just one of many possible ways to draft a whistleblower policy.

It should be noted that there are literally dozens of federal, state, and local laws that impose document retention periods on corporations. These laws are constantly changing and new laws are being added each year. Therefore, as a practical matter, it is next to impossible to completely catalog all of the document retention time periods that might apply to a nonprofit entity and then follow each of those laws to the letter. The sample below covers only the most common types of documents that might be found in a nonprofit organization and contains document retention time periods that may exceed that required by the law. Consult with legal counsel in developing your own document retention policy.

RECORD RETENTION AND DOCUMENT DESTRUCTION POLICY

POLICY PURPOSE

This policy covers all documents (including e-mail messages and electronic documents) created or received by [NONPROFIT NAME]. The policy is designed to ensure compliance with federal and state laws and regulations, to reduce the risk of accidental destruction of records earlier than intended, and to facilitate operations by promoting efficiency and freeing up valuable storage space.

Unless a specific federal or state law provides for a longer or shorter retention period than the ones specified below, [NONPROFIT NAME] follows the general document retention procedures outlined below to the extent feasible. However, no adverse inference is to be drawn from an inadvertent failure to retain a document in accordance with the guidelines below. Documents that are not listed below, but are substantially similar to those listed in the schedule, will be retained for the appropriate length of time.

Corporate Records

Annual Reports to Secretary of State/Attorney General	Permanent
Articles of Incorporation	Permanent
Board Meeting and Board Committee Minutes	Permanent
Board Policies/Resolutions	Permanent
Bylaws	Permanent
Construction Documents	Permanent
Fixed Asset Records	Permanent
IRS Application for Tax-Exempt Status (Form 1023)	Permanent
IRS Determination Letter	Permanent

State Sales Tax Exemption Letter	Permanent
Contracts (after expiration)	7 years
Correspondence (general)	3 years

Accounting and Corporate Tax Records

Annual Audits and Financial Statements	Permanent
Depreciation Schedules	Permanent
IRS Form 990 Information Returns	Permanent
General Ledgers	7 years
Business Expense Records	7 years
IRS Forms 1099	7 years
Journal Entries	7 years
Invoices	7 years
Sales Records	5 years
Petty Cash Vouchers	3 years
Cash Receipts	3 years
Credit Card Receipts	3 years

Bank Records

Check Registers	7 years
Bank Deposit Slips	7 years
Bank Statements and Reconciliation	7 years
Electronic Fund Transfer Documents	7 years

Payroll and Employment Tax Records

Payroll Registers	Permanent
State Unemployment Tax Records	Permanent
Earnings Records	7 years
Garnishment Records	7 years

Payroll Tax Returns	7 years
W-2 Statements	7 years

Employee Records

Employment and Termination Agreements	Permanent
Retirement and Pension Plan Documents	Permanent
Records Relating to Promotion, Demotion, or Discharge	7 years after termination
Accident Reports and Worker's Compensation Records	5 years
Salary Schedules	5 years
Employment Applications	3 years
I-9 Forms	3 years after termination
Time Cards	2 years

Donor and Grant Records

Donor Records and Acknowledgment Letters	7 years
Grant Applications and Contracts	7 years after completion

Legal, Insurance, and Safety Records

Appraisals	Permanent
Copyright Registrations	Permanent
Insurance Policies	Permanent
Real Estate Documents	Permanent
Stock and Bond Records	Permanent
Trademark Registrations	Permanent
Leases	6 years after expiration
OSHA Documents	5 years
General Contracts	3 years after termination

ELECTORNIC DOCUMENTS AND RECORDS

Electronic documents will be retained as if they were paper documents. Therefore, any electronic files, including records of donations made online, that fall into one of the document types on the above schedule will be maintained for the appropriate amount of time. If a user has sufficient reason to keep an e-mail message, the message should be printed in hard copy and kept in the appropriate file or moved to an "archive" computer file folder. Backup and recovery methods will be tested on a regular basis.

DOCUMENT DESTRUCTION AND EXCEPTIONS

The Executive Director is responsible for the ongoing process of identifying its records, which have met the required retention period, and overseeing their destruction. Destruction of financial and personnel-related documents will be accomplished by shredding. Notwithstanding the normal document destruction schedule of the association, document destruction will be suspended immediately in the following circumstances:

(a) where the information has been subpoenaed in a civil or criminal case, or is the subject of an information request letter from a government agency;

(b) where the information relates to civil or criminal litigation against the Association or a subsidiary that is either pending, imminent, or contemplated;

(c) where destruction of the information would impede, obstruct, or influence the administration of any matter within the jurisdiction of the federal government, where such matter is pending, imminent or contemplated, or;

(d) where the association's general counsel places a "legal hold" on any document for any reason.

Destruction will be reinstated upon conclusion of the investigation or lawsuit, but only after consultation between the Executive Director and the organization's legal counsel.

COMPLIANCE AND SANCTIONS

Failure on the part of employees to follow this policy can result in possible civil and criminal sanctions against [NONPROFIT NAME] and possible disciplinary action against responsible individuals. The Executive Director will periodically review these procedures with legal counsel or the organization's certified public accountant to ensure that they are in compliance with new or revised laws and regulations.

APPENDIX 5

FREQUENTLY ASKED QUESTIONS

1. **Question:** What is the best method for drafting bylaws?

   Answer: The ideal method is to involve your board in the process. Do research, discuss the options for the various clauses, and together decide how you want your board to govern. Then have a lawyer review your draft to ensure that you are in compliance with state law and that you don't have contradictory statements in your bylaws.

   Another recommended method is to hire a knowledgeable lawyer and to explain to that person the type of governance structure you would like. Hiring a lawyer costs money, but it does save large amounts of time and is much more likely to ensure that the end product satisfies state law, is internally consistent, and is less ambiguous. If your organization cannot afford a lawyer, then try to form a very small bylaws committee of people who have experience serving on other nonprofit boards and dealing with bylaws issues

2. **Question:** The board suddenly decided to "clarify" the bylaws, just before an election, which made two of the three candidates running for president ineligible. Is there any kind of ruling that would cover this?

   Answer: Ideally, bylaws should be so clearly written in the first place that the qualifications to run for elected office would never need to be "clarified." However, where there is ambiguity, the board chair (preferably with the help of legal counsel) should interpret the bylaws. In some cases, the interpretation of a clause will depend on knowing the long-standing (historical) practice of the organization with respect to the issue in question, since long-standing practice is often a good indicator of what a bylaws clause was intended to mean.

3. **Question:** In revising the bylaws, I accidentally left out a sentence referring to the size of the board. How would we go about correcting this omission?

   Answer: If the missing sentence was in a "redlined" discussion draft of the bylaws that was reviewed by the board and that was not the subject of any objection, but the sentence was later accidentally deleted in the final "clean" version of the bylaws that was voted on by the board, many organizations would treat that as a mere "scrivener's error" and would consider the missing sentence to have been approved. But if the bylaws committee completely forgot to put the sentence into the bylaws amendments in the first place so that it was never part of any discussion draft that was reviewed by the board, then the best solution is to go through the bylaws amendment process a second time to add the missing sentence. This question demonstrates how important it is to act with great care and attention to detail when amending bylaws.

4. **Question:** Several months ago I came across an old copy of our bylaws that's different from the one we're using as the ruling document. There's one major difference between them addressing who can amend the bylaws. How do we determine which copy is the right one?

   Answer: This problem can easily be avoided if each new version of the bylaws is dated with its effective date somewhere on the document. In the absence of a date, the next logical step is to review old board minutes to try to determine when the particular clause in question may have been amended and how that clause should currently read. If minutes do not resolve the issues, a final option is to discuss the different bylaws versions with any bylaws committee the organization might have and with any current or past officers and directors with historical knowledge about the bylaws to see if anyone can remember which version is current.

5. **Question:** It's my understanding that the bylaws are voted on as a whole, and then they pass or don't. What happens if one section is approved and another isn't? Do we cut and paste our bylaws?

Answer: While initial bylaws for a new nonprofit are typically voted on as a whole, subsequent bylaws changes often focus on just a single paragraph or sentence, unless the organization has gone through a major restructuring and has decided to rewrite the entire bylaws. In any case, the board generally has discretion on now to handle the amendment process. One option is to require substantially revised bylaws to be amended as a whole, meaning that a person casts a vote either for or against the entire package of amendments. However, if insufficient votes exist to approve the new bylaws, then the old bylaws remain in place, which may hamper the organization's progress.

A second option is to offer the bylaws as a whole, but then allow piecemeal amendments to any of the clauses to be made by the board (or from the floor of a membership meeting if bylaws are being approved by the members). There are complex rules for allowing such piecemeal amendments that are described in the various parliamentary authorities (such as *Robert's Rules of Order*), so to the extent an organization has adopted such parliamentary rules, they would need to be consulted. One problem with allowing last-minute bylaws amendments to be made from the floor is that there is extremely limited time for thoughtful discussion on the amendment. Consequently, it is possible that an oral amendment that seems reasonable on its face might end up being inconsistent with some other part of the bylaws upon reflection later. Therefore, allowing piecemeal and last-minute floor amendments to bylaws must be done with great caution and should generally be avoided. This question raises the importance of having major bylaws revisions "vetted" in advance by all major stakeholders and with plenty of opportunity for changes to be proposed and commented on well in advance so that when the time finally comes for a formal vote, the bylaws have a high likelihood of passing without further amendments or debate.

6. **Question:** A lawyer put in our new bylaws that the board president shall be the chief executive officer of the corporation. The board president contends that the executive director is the chief executive officer. Who is right?

   Answer: In the absence of other higher authority, the bylaws always prevail. Thus, if the bylaws say that the president is the chief executive officer, then that is the case, even if that designation may not match reality. The chief executive officer is normally supposed to be the operational leader responsible for the day-to-day control of the organization and its staff, although it is not essential that the person's title have the words "chief executive" in it. In organizations that have no paid staff and where the entity is run entirely by a volunteer board and officers, it is quite possible for the person who is president to also be designated as the chief executive officer too. However, in organizations that have paid employees on staff who run the organization on a day-to-day basis, it is much more common for the senior staff person (which might be the executive director in the above example) to be designated as the chief executive officer. If the bylaws indicate that the president is the chief executive officer while in reality the day-to-day control of the organization is in the hands of some other senior staff person, then it would be prudent to amend the bylaws.

7. **Question:** Are there any specific issues that need to be addressed in a religious nonprofit that are different from other nonprofits?

   Answer: No, not really. While some churches may create a governance structure that contains officer titles and committee names that are unique to the organization, the vast majority of nonprofit organizations (including those with a religious mission) face the same governance and bylaws issues. And if the organization is incorporated, it would be governed by the same state law as any other nonprofit formed in that state. Thus, it is a misconception to believe that a religious nonprofit needs radically different articles of incorporation, bylaws, and governance policies than does any other type of nonprofit.

8. **Question:** Since our bylaws state that elections take place in December, would we have to amend our bylaws before we could actually change the election date?

   Answer: If at all possible, bylaws should not specify the exact month that an election or other event will occur because doing so provides no flexibility. But if the bylaws mandate December elections, and if you want to avoid a possible legal challenge to an election that is held in another month, then it would be prudent to amend the bylaws before holding an election in another month. However, in some organizations where the bylaws state a particular month for elections or a particular month for the membership meeting, the clause is often viewed as aspirational so that if business necessity, weather, or other factors push the election or meeting to a different month, there is seldom any objection from the board or the members. Still, the better practice is not to specify a particular month in the bylaws.

9. **Question:** When a nonprofit is faced with a governance issue (such as a question on how to remove a director from office), where should it look for the answer? Should it look at the bylaws, a parliamentary authority such as *Robert's Rules of Order,* the articles of incorporation, or state law?

   Answer: State nonprofit corporation law is always the highest authority and is always the first place to look for the answer to a governance issue. Next in line would be the articles of incorporation, although they should not have much governance detail in them. The bylaws are the next place to look, and, presumably, most governance details that are not mandated by state law are set forth in the bylaws. Only if the answer to the issue is not covered by one of the above authorities, and only if the bylaws indicate that some parliamentary authority has been adopted by the organization, would you look to that parliamentary authority.

10. **Question:** If the board of a nonprofit corporation desires to amend its bylaws, when does that amendment have to be filed with the state?

Answer: Bylaws (including amendments) are never filed with the state. Because no state official ever compares a nonprofit's bylaws to the provisions of state law, it is possible for a board to have bylaws that violate the law and not realize it until such time as adverse action is taken against an officer or director and that person hires a lawyer.

11. **Question:** A member of the public called our nonprofit and demanded to have a copy of our bylaws. The caller claims that federal law requires us to make all of our key documents available to the public. What should we do?

Answer: While the Form 990 information return and the original IRS tax exemption application (Form 1023) are required to be made public under certain circumstances, the bylaws are not required by federal law to be made public. Therefore, nonprofits have discretion as to whether to provide the document or not.

SUGGESTED RESOURCES

BoardSource. *The Nonprofit Board Answer Book: A Practical Guide for Board Members and Chief Executives, Second Edition.* San Francisco: Jossey-Bass, 2007.
This book provides a wealth of information about board structure and process, meetings, board composition, orientation, board-staff relations, financial management, and much more. The book offers insight gained from hundreds of board self-assessments and questions and challenges from thousands of nonprofit leaders. Written in an easy-to-use question-and-answer format, it includes action steps, examples, and worksheets.

BoardSource. *Nonprofit Governance Index 2007.*
This paper summarizes findings from a survey of chief executives and board members of nonprofit organizations in the United States. Available at:
www.boardsource.org/dl.asp?document_id=553

Flynn, Outi. *Meeting, and Exceeding Expectations: A Guide to Successful Nonprofit Board Meetings, Second Edition.* Washington, D.C., BoardSource, 2009.
This book provides ready-to-use information that will help your board members provide the valuable input that will propel your organization to greatness. This must-have resource poses critical questions, provides easy-to-implement answers, suggests tools, and clarifies legal and ethical expectations. It also shows you how to insert some fun into your meetings. It is designed for chief executives, board members, senior staff, and any other participants involved in board meetings.

Hopkins, Bruce R. *Legal Responsibilities of Nonprofit Boards, Second Edition.* Washington, DC: BoardSource, 2009.
Written for the reader without a legal background, this booklet translates technical law into everyday language to help board members understand their legal responsibilities — including the duties of care, loyalty, and obedience.

Hopkins, Bruce R. *Starting and Managing a Nonprofit Organization – A Legal Guide, Fourth Edition.* Hoboken, NJ: John Wiley & Sons, Inc., 2005.
Answers all the basic questions you need to know in forming and operating a nonprofit organization. Mr. Hopkins has written more books on nonprofit law than just about anyone, and he has the ability to make even the most complex concepts understandable.

Hopkins, Bruce R., and D. Benson Tesdahl. *Intermediate Sanctions – Curbing Nonprofit Abuse.* Hoboken, NJ: John Wiley & Sons, Inc., 1997.
The only book of its kind discussing in detail the Intermediate Sanctions Law (Internal Revenue Code section 4958) governing compensation and other financial arrangements with nonprofit officers, directors, and senior executives. It is a useful guide for nonprofits desiring to set executive compensation policies.

Kirschten, Barbara. *Nonprofit Corporation Forms Handbook.* Eagan, MN: West, 2009.
This handbook contains useful articles of incorporation and bylaws samples with citations to state law for a limited number of states.

Lawrence, Barbara, and Outi Flynn. *The Nonprofit Policy Sampler, Second Edition.* Washington, DC: BoardSource, 2006.
This compilation contains 241 samples of nonprofit policies covering 48 different issues areas.

Mancuso, Anthony. *How to Form a Nonprofit Corporation.* Berkeley, CA: Nolo Press, 2002.
This complete guide contains simple information, with examples on how to prepare articles, bylaws, and minutes for a nonprofit organization.

Robert's Rules of Order, Newly Revised (10th Edition)
www.robertsrules.com and *The Standard Code of Parliamentary Procedure* (4th Edition) (also known as Sturgis Standard Code of Parliamentary Procedure) Available at:
http://ebooks.ebookmall.com/ebook/137692-ebook.htm.
These resources are two of the more commonly used parliamentary guides for conducting corporate meetings. However, they are not "the law" and they must be used with caution and only after first reviewing state law and the bylaws, which always have precedence.

The Sarbanes-Oxley Act and Implications for Nonprofit Organizations. Washington, DC: BoardSource and Independent Sector, 2006. Available at:
www.boardsource.org/clientfiles/sarbanes-oxley.pdf
This white paper explains those few portions of the Sarbanes-Oxley Act that apply to nonprofit corporations and explains how other parts of the Act can still be followed by analogy in an effort to make nonprofits good corporate citizens.

ABOUT THE AUTHOR

D. Benson Tesdahl is a senior attorney with the law firm of Powers, Pyles, Sutter & Verville, P.C. in Washington, DC. He holds a bachelor of science degree from the U.S. Military Academy at West Point and a master of science degree in Systems Management from the University of Southern California. He earned his J.D. degree from the University of Oregon Law School, where he was selected to the national law school honor society, Order of the Coif, and was an associate editor of the *Oregon Law Review*. He later earned a master of laws degree (LL.M.) in taxation, with distinction, from Georgetown University Law Center.

Mr. Tesdahl has specialized in the representation of tax-exempt organizations for more than 20 years. His clients include all types of nonprofit entities, including charitable and educational organizations, trade and professional organizations, hospitals and other healthcare entities, and religious organizations. His practice encompasses the full spectrum of legal issues applicable to tax-exempt organizations, including incorporating and obtaining tax exemption for new organizations, forming for-profit and nonprofit subsidiaries, providing advice on bylaws and governance issues, and providing advice on the unrelated business income rules and lobbying and political activity restrictions. He also advises on collateral areas of law, including contract law (with exceptional experience in the unique issues surrounding hotel and meeting contracts), personnel law, and copyright and trademark law. He has assisted many nonprofit organizations with their strategic planning and in finding innovative ways of improving their corporate sponsorship income.

Mr. Tesdahl has been an adjunct professor of law at Georgetown University Law Center, where he taught an advanced seminar on tax-exempt organizations as part of the university's graduate tax program. He currently serves on the Council of Editorial Advisors of BoardSource. He is co-author of *Intermediate Sanctions: Curbing Nonprofit Abuse,* published by John Wiley & Sons, and has written chapters for two treatises on nonprofit organizations, also published by Wiley. For more than four years, he wrote a monthly tax column for the *Exempt Organization Tax Review,* published by Tax Analysts, and he continues to serve on its editorial board. He also writes a regular legal column for *Successful Meetings* Magazine.

Mr. Tesdahl is a member of the American Bar Association's Committee on Exempt Organizations, the Professional Convention Management Association, and of the American Society of Association Executives. He is admitted to practice in the District of Columbia, Washington State, and the United States Supreme Court.